Contents

Introduction

Outline of the course

Junior Certificate Home Economics is offered at Ordinary and Higher Level. The course consists of two sections:

- A **common course** of five areas of study
- One compulsory **project** from a choice of three options

The **common course** consists of the following five units of study:

- Food studies and culinary skills
- Consumer studies
- Social and health studies
- Resource management and home studies
- Textile studies

The course is **examined** with:

- A **written** examination
- A **practical** test (Food and Culinary Skills Examination)
- A **project** chosen from one of the following areas:
  1 Childcare
  2 Design and craftwork
  3 Textile skills

How the course is dealt with in the book

This revision guide is focused on the written examination. It is divided into **three** parts:
1 A topics section
2 An examination section
3 A study plan

In the **topics section** each of the five areas of study are outlined.
Each section includes:

- Learning objectives
- Text summaries with highlighted key points
- Sample questions

The sample questions are long questions from Ordinary and Higher Level exam papers. Ordinary Level questions have been included to offer more scope for practice. You could try to answer at Higher Level standard.

The **examination section** covers:
- The structure of the written exam
- Examination tips
- Common pitfalls
- Learning tips

It also contains:
- A breakdown of subjects from previous state examinations
- A past exam paper complete with sample answers and marking scheme

The **study plan** provides a template which allows you to organise your study. You can fill in the times and dates on which you will revise each part of the course. In a 'night before' section you can list the key areas to be included in a final revision.

Preparing for the written exam

1 **Choose** the **unit** and **chapter** which you intend to revise
2 **Study** the **learning objectives** of this section, e.g.:
   - Outline the functions of …
   - Name the sources of …
   - List the factors to be considered …
   - Outline the importance of …
   - Describe the features of …
   - List the reasons why …
   - Outline the effects of …
   - Give guidelines for …
   - Sketch …

3 **Make notes.** On the following pages three different methods of making notes are described. Choose the method which best suits the topic

(a) Draw up a **table** and include all the important points of information. Use clear headings as shown in the example below.

Macronutrients

Nutrient	Classification	Sources	Functions	RDA	Current Dietary Guidelines	Health Problems
Protein	High biological value Low biological value					
Fat						
Carbohydrates						

(b) Create a **web diagram** or **map**.

Write the key word in the middle of the diagram and link it with each of the subsections as shown in the example and fill in any information relating to this section.

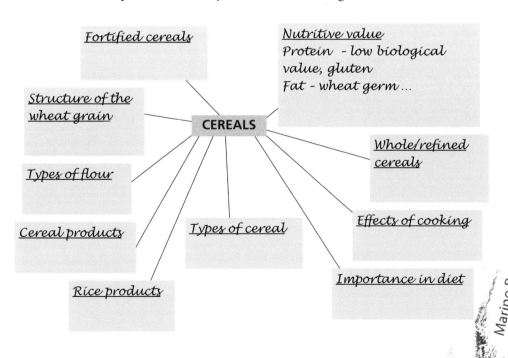

Fortified cereals

Nutritive value
Protein - low biological value, gluten
Fat - wheat germ ...

Structure of the wheat grain

CEREALS

Whole/refined cereals

Types of flour

Cereal products

Types of cereal

Effects of cooking

Rice products

Importance in diet

Marino Branch
Brainse Marglann Mhuirine
Tel: 8336297

(c) Draw an **information tree**.

Write the key headings on the left side of the page. Draw branches from each heading and list the relevant points as shown in the example below.

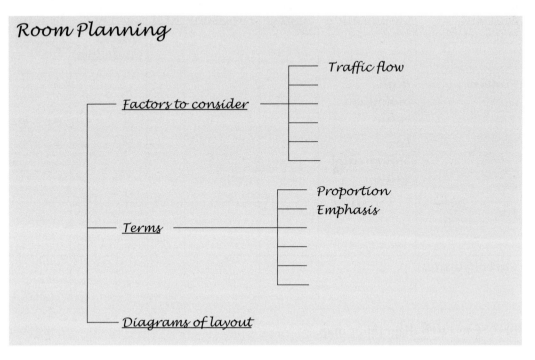

Room Planning

Factors to consider — Traffic flow

Terms — Proportion / Emphasis

Diagrams of layout

4 **Use the study plan to record the dates** on which you will revise the section again. Each section should be revised several times

5 **File your notes** carefully and **review them** regularly so that you are very familiar with them. This will help you to remember the information and it will improve your confidence as you approach the exam

Topics section

- **Unit 1** Food studies and culinary skills

- **Unit 2** Consumer studies

- **Unit 3** Social and health studies

- **Unit 4** Resource management and home studies

- **Unit 5** Textile studies

●●●**Learning Objectives**

In this chapter you will learn to:
1 List the nutrients
2 Classify the macronutrients
3 Give the sources, functions, RDA and health problems associated with each nutrient

Functions of food

- Food helps the body to **grow**
- Food provides the body with **energy** and **warmth**
- Food **protects** the body against disease

Factors affecting food choice

- Cost
- Availability
- Lifestyle or eating patterns of a family or an individual
- Culture, such as festive occasions, or religion
- Nutritive value
- The senses

Points to note

The four tastes sensed by the taste buds are **sweet, sour, bitter** and **salty**.

Points to note

Staple foods are those which are plentiful and most commonly eaten in a country.

Nutrients

There are six groups of nutrients:
- Protein
- Fat
- Carbohydrates
- Vitamins
- Minerals
- Water

Macronutrients and micronutrients

- Nutrients needed in **large amounts** by the body are called **macronutrients**
- Nutrients needed in very **small amounts** by the body are called **micronutrients**

Macronutrients	Micronutrients
Protein	Vitamins
Fat	Minerals
Carbohydrates	

Protein

Composition of protein

- Proteins are made up of amino acids
- Amino acids consist of the elements carbon, oxygen, hydrogen and nitrogen

Classification and sources of protein

High Biological Value Protein	Low Biological Value Protein
Meat	Peas
Fish	Beans
Eggs	Lentils
Milk and dairy produce, e.g. cheese and yoghurt	Nuts
Soya beans	Whole cereals

Functions of protein

Protein is needed in the body for the following reasons:

- Growth
- Repair of damaged cells
- Formation of hormones and enzymes
- A source of heat and energy

Recommended dietary allowance

The recommended dietary allowance (RDA) of protein depends on your weight. **Adults need 1g of protein for every kilogram that they weigh.** Therefore, if you weigh 60kg, you need 60g of protein each day.

Fats

Composition of fat

- Fats are made from **fatty acids** and **glycerol**
- Glycerol and fatty acids contain the elements carbon, hydrogen and oxygen

Classification and sources of fats

Saturated Fats	Unsaturated Fats
Butter	Sunflower oil
Meat	Corn oil
Milk and cream	Olive oil
Cheese	Fish oils, e.g. cod liver oil
Egg yolk	Oily fish, e.g. mackerel and salmon
Suet	Nuts
Lard	Avocados
Dripping	Seeds
	Whole cereals
	Polyunsaturated margarine, e.g. Flora

Functions of fats

- A source of heat and energy
- A source of fat soluble vitamins A, D, E and K
- Fat under the skin insulates the body
- Fats protect delicate organs
- Fats give a feeling of fullness

Fats in the diet

- **Too much fat** in the diet can lead to **overweight and obesity**
- **Too much saturated fat** in the diet is associated with **heart disease and stroke**

Carbohydrates

Composition of carbohydrates

- Carbohydrates are made up of simple sugars called **glucose**
- **Glucose** units are joined together to form **starch**
- Carbohydrates contain the elements carbon, hydrogen and oxygen

Classification and sources of carbohydrates

Sugars	Starches	Dietary Fibre
Sugar	Cereals	Vegetables
Fruit (fresh and dried)	Potatoes	Fruit
Milk	Root vegetables	Whole cereals
Honey	Pulse vegetables	
Soft drinks		
Cakes		
Biscuits		
Jam		
Ice cream		

Functions of carbohydrates

- Sugars and starchy foods provide heat and energy
- **Fibre** helps to move food along the intestine by muscular contractions called **peristalsis**
- Fibre gives a feeling of fullness

Fibre

- When cereals are **refined** or processed, the fibre is removed
- White flour is an example of a **refined cereal**
- **Whole cereals (unrefined)** are better for the body because they **contain fibre**

Recommended dietary allowance

The RDA for fibre is 30g for an average person.

Vitamins

Classification of vitamins

Vitamins are divided into two groups:

- **Water soluble**
- **Fat soluble**

Water Soluble Vitamins	Fat Soluble Vitamins
Vitamin B group	Vitamin A
Vitamin C	Vitamin D
	Vitamin E
	Vitamin K

Water soluble vitamins

Vitamin	Functions	Sources	Deficiency Disease
C (ascorbic acid)	• Necessary for general health • Necessary for healthy skin, gums and blood vessels • Helps the body to absorb iron • Helps the formation of connective tissue	Fresh fruit and vegetables, e.g. blackcurrants, kiwi fruit, green peppers, rosehips, citrus fruits, strawberries, spinach, cabbage, broccoli	• Scurvy • Delayed healing of wounds • Anaemia (because iron is not absorbed)
B group	• Controls the release of energy from food • Necessary for healthy nerves • Helps growth	Meat, fish, cheese, eggs, wholemeal bread, cereals, nuts, pulses, yeast	• Beri-beri (a nerve disease) • Pellagra (tongue and skin become sore)

Recommended dietary allowance

The RDA for vitamin C is 50–60g per day.

Fat soluble vitamins

Vitamin	Functions	Sources	Deficiency Disease
A (Carotene is converted to vitamin A in the body.)	• Growth • Healthy eyes • Healthy skin • Healthy lining membranes, e.g. in nose and throat	Fish liver oils, oily fish, offal, butter, margarine, eggs **Carotene** in carrots, apricots, tomatoes, dark green vegetables	• Retarded growth • Night blindness • Dry lining membranes • Rough dry skin
D	• Helps the absorption of calcium for healthy bones and teeth	Sunshine Cod liver oil, oily fish, eggs, offal, margarine	• Rickets in children • Unhealthy teeth
E	• An antioxidant thought to reduce the incidence of ageing and cancer • Healthy red blood cells	Sunflower seeds, margarine, eggs, cereals	• Anaemia in newborn babies
K	• Necessary for blood to clot	Made by bacteria in the intestine Green vegetables, cereals	• Blood does not clot, causing bleeding and haemorrhage

Recommended dietary allowance

- The RDA for vitamin A is 700µg (microgram) per day for teenagers
- The RDA for vitamin D is 15µg per day for teenagers

Minerals

Mineral	Functions	Sources	Deficiency Disease
Calcium	• Healthy bones and teeth • Needed to clot blood	Milk, cheese, yoghurt, tinned fish, green vegetables, fortified flour, hard water	• Rickets in children • Osteoporosis in adults • Unhealthy teeth
Iron	• Necessary to form haemoglobin in red blood cells	Red meat, meat products, eggs, whole cereals, green vegetables, pulses	• Tiredness • Weakness • Anaemia caused by lack of haemoglobin in the blood
Sodium	• Controls water balance in the body	Table salt, bacon, processed meats, snack foods, butter, cheese	• Muscular cramps
Fluoride	• Healthy teeth	Drinking water, fish	• Tooth decay

Points to note

Minerals which are needed in very small amounts are called **trace minerals**.

Recommended dietary allowance

Mineral	Recommended Dietary Allowance
Calcium	1200mg (milligram)
Iron	14mg
Sodium	1.6g

Water

Lack of water in the diet causes **dehydration**.

Functions of water

- Water satisfies thirst
- It helps digestion
- It helps remove waste from the body
- It is a source of minerals such as fluoride and calcium
- It is an essential part of all body fluids and body cells

Energy

Oxidation

Oxygen burns up food in the body cells, releasing the energy. This is called **oxidation**.

Measuring energy

The amount of energy in food is measured in units called **kilocalories** (kcal) or **kilojoules** (kJ).

Points to note

1kcal = 4.2kJ

Factors which influence a person's energy requirements

- **Size:** Big people need more energy than small people
- **Activity:** Active people need more energy than inactive people
- **Gender:** Males generally need more energy than females

- **Climate:** People in cold climates need more energy in order to keep warm than people in warm climates
- **Age:** Adults need more energy than young children
- **Pregnancy:** Pregnant and breastfeeding women need extra energy

Energy balance

Energy balance means that **energy input** (energy from our food) **must be equal to energy output** (energy which we use) in order to have the correct body weight.

Empty kilocalories

Some foods provide energy but do not contain any other nutrients. Therefore they provide **empty kilocalories**. Fizzy drinks and table sugar contain empty kilocalories.

Sample exam question

Question

(a) (i) Plan and set out a menu for a two-course main meal for yourself and three friends that can be prepared and served in one hour.
   (ii) Evaluate the nutritive value of the meal.
(b) (i) State the importance of including protein in the diet of teenagers.
   (ii) List four good sources of protein in the diet.
(c) Explain any two of the following:
   (i) amino acid; (ii) high biological value; (iii) textured vegetable protein.

(1998, HL)

1.2 A balanced diet

●●● **Learning Objectives**

In this chapter you will learn to:
1. Explain the terms 'balanced diet' and 'food pyramid'
2. Name the four food groups and summarise the recommendations from each food group for different age groups
3. Summarise the guidelines for balanced eating for babies, young children, adolescents, adults, pregnant and breastfeeding women, the elderly and convalescents

- **A balanced diet** contains all the nutrients the body needs in the correct proportion. It provides all the body's requirements for growth and development
- Of all the foods we eat, **half** should be made up of carbohydrates, **one-third** should be made up of fats and **one-sixth** should be made up of protein
- Fibre, minerals, vitamins and water should also be included

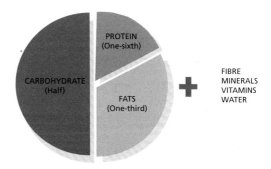

Points to note

There are no good or bad foods – only good or bad diets.

The four food groups

Food Group	Functions
Cereal and potato group	Provides energy, fibre and B vitamins
Fruit and vegetable group	Provides minerals, vitamins, energy and fibre
Milk group	Provides protein, fat, calcium, vitamins
Meat group	Provides protein, fat, iron, vitamin B

A good way of getting a balanced diet is by eating a certain number of portions each day from each of the **four food groups**.

Meat Group	Fruit and Vegetables Group	Cereal and Potato Group	Milk Group
Protein foods • Meat and fish are good sources of protein for body building • Vegetarians can get protein from foods such as lentils, beans, eggs and cheese	**Vitamins and minerals** • Needed to supply a variety of vitamins and some minerals • Fresh or frozen vegetables are better than tinned • Fresh fruit and vegetables provide fibre to avoid constipation	**Energy foods** • Keep you active • Wholemeal bread is better than white • Wholemeal bread provides fibre and small amounts of protein, vitamins and minerals • The amount of food required from this group depends on weight and age	**Dairy products** • These are rich in calcium and protein • Calcium is important to build strong bones and teeth • Milk also supplies vitamin B_2, needed to help release energy from food, and small amounts of other vitamins and minerals
Meat etc. One serving/item consists of: • 2oz (60g) cooked lean meat or poultry • 3oz (90g) fish • 2 eggs • 2oz (60g) cheddar-type cheese • 2 large tbsp boiled peas/beans • 3oz (90g) nuts	**Fruit/Vegetable** One serving/item consists of: • Average serving of cooked fruit • Large serving of cooked veg or salad • Medium-sized fresh fruit • Small glass of fruit juice	**Bread and cereals** (preferably wholegrain) One serving/item consists of: • 1 slice of bread • Bowl of cereal • 1 large tbsp of boiled rice or pasta • 1 medium potato	**Milk products** (preferably low fat) One serving/item consists of: • Glass of milk • Carton of yoghurt • Average bowl of milk pudding, e.g. rice pudding • 1oz (30g) cheddar-type cheese
Recommended servings per day: (1) 2 items (2) 2 items (3) 2 items (4) 3 items (5) 3 items	**Recommended servings per day:** (1) 5 items (2) 5 items (3) 5 items (4) 5 items (5) 5 items	**Recommended servings per day:** (1) 4 items (2) 6 items (3) 6 items (4) 6 items (5) 6 items	**Recommended servings per day:** (1) 3 items (2) 5 items (3) 3 items (4) 5 items (5) 5 items

(1) child, (2) teenager, (3) adult, (4) pregnant woman, (5) nursing mother

The food pyramid

The **food pyramid** is another way of representing the food groups.

Use the Food Pyramid to plan your healthy food choices

Very small amounts
Choose oil, margarine or low-fat spreads labelled 'High in Polyunsaturates' or 'High in Monounsaturates' which are healthier for your heart. Use small amounts.

Meat, poultry, fish, eggs, beans and peas
Choose any 2
Choose 3 servings during pregnancy.

Milk, cheese and yoghurt
Choose any 3
Choose 5 servings for teenagers, or for pregnant or breastfeeding mothers.

Fruit and vegetables
Choose any 5
Choose green, leafy vegetables, oranges or orange juice most days.

Bread, cereal and potatoes
Choose any 6 or more
Choose high fibre cereals and breads often. If you do a lot of physical activity you may need up to 12 servings.

Drink at least 8 glasses of water a day or water based drinks like tea, coffee and diluted drinks

Balanced eating for different age groups

Our food needs change as we grow from infancy to adulthood.

Remember ...
... 5 points for each.

Babies

1 **Breastfeeding** is recommended as it contains all the nutrients in proportion to the baby's needs. Dried cow's **milk formulas** are available as an alternative

2 **Avoid** giving **skimmed milk** to babies as it lacks fat and fat soluble vitamins

3 Babies are **weaned** (introduced to solid foods) at four to six months

4 **Do not** add sugar or salt to a baby's food. **Do not** give spicy or fatty foods to babies

5 From eight months on, a baby should be eating a good **varied diet**, with plentiful supplies of all the essential nutrients

Young children

1 Young children **grow rapidly**, therefore their needs for protein, calcium and energy are high

2 **Fruit and vegetables** provide vitamin C, iron and fibre

3 **Healthy eating habits** should be developed from an early age and food 'fads' should be discouraged

4 Children need more **frequent meals** or nutritious snacks because of their small stomachs

5 They should **not eat** high-fat, salty or sugary snacks in between meals

Adolescents

1 There is a rapid **growth spurt** among boys and girls between the ages of 10 and 15 years. Their **energy requirements** are high

2 **Calcium** and **iron** are particularly important for the development of strong bones and teeth and to prevent anaemia

3 Teenagers should eat a good **variety** of foods and balance their food intake with **physical activity**. Plenty of fruit and vegetables, wholegrain cereals and dairy products should be included

4 Active teenagers should get their energy from **starchy carbohydrates** rather than sugars or fats. Excessive amounts of soft drinks, crisps, burgers, chips and chocolate may cause weight problems or worsen skin problems

5 A **doctor's advice** should be sought and followed before starting on any type of diet, such as vegetarianism

Adults

1 Adults' needs vary depending on **gender** and **level of activity**. Males require more energy than females because of their larger size. Also a **manual** worker requires more energy than a **sedentary** worker because physical activity burns up more energy

2 Adults should eat a good **variety** of foods, ensuring they get their daily requirements from all the food groups

3 Adults should **avoid** too much **saturated fat, sugar and salt** to reduce the risk of weight problems, coronary heart disease and high blood pressure

4 Adequate **fibre** intake will prevent bowel disorders and control appetite

5 Women should ensure high intakes of **calcium** to reduce the risk of osteoporosis and **iron** to prevent anaemia

Pregnant and breastfeeding women

1 During pregnancy and breastfeeding, a woman must eat a **well-balanced diet** to provide all the essential nutrients for her own health and her baby's growth and development. Breastfeeding mothers should avoid nicotine and alcohol and drink coffee in moderation

2 **Protein, calcium, phosphorus, vitamins A and D** are all needed for the growth of the foetus and the development of bones and teeth

3 **Iron** and **vitamin C** are needed to prevent anaemia and fight infections. **Folic acid** should be taken before and during pregnancy to prevent spina bifida and other neural tube defects

4 **Fibre-rich foods** and plenty of fluids are required to prevent constipation, which can be quite common during pregnancy

5 Pregnant women are advised to **avoid** unpasteurised cheeses, cook-chill foods, alcohol and cigarettes, spicy or rich foods, strong tea and coffee

---

Points to note

Manual occupations are those which require physical strength and activity, e.g. farmer, builder, aerobics instructor. **Sedentary** occupations require little physical effort, e.g. teacher, secretary, computer programmer.

REVISE WISE POINTS TO NOTE

Elderly people

1 Elderly people need **less energy** per day as they tend to be less physically active
2 **Easily digested protein** foods, such as chicken and white fish, are needed for repair and growth of new cells
3 Fresh fruit and vegetables will provide **fibre and vitamin C** to prevent constipation and to fight against infection
4 **Calcium** strengthens teeth and bones and **iron** is needed to prevent anaemia
5 Elderly people should **cut down** on **saturated fats and salt** to reduce the risk of heart disease and stroke

Convalescents/Invalids

1 **Energy foods** should be kept to a **minimum** as the convalescent may be confined to bed
2 Follow **doctor's advice** regarding suitable foods. All meals should be prepared and served hygienically
3 Foods should be **light** and **easy to digest**. Avoid spicy or fatty foods or reheated foods
4 **Stewing, steaming, boiling and baking** are suitable methods of cooking
5 Ensure **plenty of fluids** are taken, especially if the patient has a fever

1.3 Special diets

●●●**Learning Objectives**

In this chapter you will learn to:
1 Outline the benefits of each special diet
2 List the foods associated with each special diet
3 Give guidelines for each special diet
4 List health problems associated with various unhealthy diets

High-fibre diet

Benefits of a high-fibre diet

- Fibre prevents constipation
- It also prevents any poisonous chemicals from building up in the body
- Fibre is useful in weight-reducing diets because it does not contain calories

Health problems associated with a low-fibre diet

- Constipation occurs when faeces (waste) become lodged in the bowel
- Bowel disease such as diverticulosis is caused by hard faeces (waste) lodging in the bowel wall. This can lead to bowel cancer
- Piles (swollen blood vessels) occur in the anus as a result of hard waste matter passing through

Guidelines to increase fibre intake

- Choose whole cereals such as wholemeal bread instead of refined cereals
- Eat high-fibre breakfast cereals
- Leave the skins on fruit and vegetables where possible
- Eat whole fruits instead of drinking fruit juices
- Include pulse vegetables in the diet
- Substitute processed snack foods with fresh or dried fruit

Low-salt diet

Health problems associated with a high-salt diet

- High blood pressure
- Coronary heart disease
- Stroke
- Fluid retention

Foods With High-Fibre Content

- Wholegrain flour
- Whole-wheat pasta
- Wholegrain cereals
- Vegetables and fruit with the skins on
- Nuts
- Seeds

Foods With High-Salt Content

- Packet and tinned soups
- Instant noodles
- Stock cubes
- Ketchup
- Sausages and burgers
- Salty savoury snacks, such as potato crisps, popcorn, salted nuts

Guidelines to reduce salt intake

- Reduce the amount of salt you add at the table and during cooking
- Use herbs, spices and pepper to flavour food instead of salt
- Choose fresh meat and vegetables instead of processed food products
- Avoid instant foods with a high-salt content
- Read food labels to check for salt or sodium. Monosodium glutamate (MSG) is also a type of salt

Low-sugar diet

Health problems associated with a high-sugar diet

- Tooth decay
- Overweight and obesity

Foods With High-Sugar Content

- Fizzy drinks   - Cakes
- Sweets   - Biscuits
- Sweet snacks   - Convenience
- Drinks sweetened   sauces such as
   with sugar   ketchup
- Sugary breakfast
   cereals

Guidelines to reduce sugar intake

- Avoid fizzy drinks, sweet snacks, drinks sweetened with sugar, sugary breakfast cereals, biscuits, cakes and convenience foods with a high-sugar content
- Reduce the amount of sugar added to food during preparation and cooking
- Use artificial sweeteners instead of sugar to sweeten foods
- Replace sweet snacks with healthier options, such as fresh fruit, vegetables, seeds and nuts

- Read food labels to identify foods containing sugar. Sucrose, fructose and glucose are various types of sugar

Obesity

Obesity means being **twenty per cent or more over the recommended weight for height**.

Causes of obesity

- **Too many calories** are consumed
- **Lack of exercise**
- Obesity can be **hereditary** in a small percentage of cases

Health problems associated with obesity

- Obese people are at risk of developing the following diseases:
  (a) Diabetes
  (b) Heart disease
  (c) Varicose veins
  (d) High blood pressure
  (e) Stroke
  (f) Gall stones
- Poor self-image

Healthy eating guidelines to reduce the risk of obesity

- Reduce calorie intake by:
  (a) Using low-fat methods of cooking such as grilling
  (b) Avoiding sugar in drinks
  (c) Removing visible fat from meat
  (d) Choosing low-fat products
  (e) Not eating between meals
- Increase high-fibre foods
- Avoid crash or fad diets
- Take more exercise to use up extra energy from food

Low fat/low cholesterol diet

Health problems associated with a high-fat diet

- Overweight and obesity
- Coronary heart disease
- Other diseases, such as diabetes, are made worse

Foods With High-Fat Content

- Butter
- Margarine
- Lard
- Cream
- Cheese
- Meat fat
- Cakes
- Biscuits
- Crisps
- Savoury snacks
- Chocolates

Coronary heart disease

Coronary heart disease occurs when the arteries of the heart become blocked with a substance called cholesterol.

Points to note

Cholesterol is a fatty substance which clings to the walls of the arteries.

Causes of heart disease

- A history of heart disease in one's family (heredity)
- A diet containing a lot of **saturated fat** can raise the amount of **cholesterol** in the blood. This leads to heart disease
- Overweight
- Lack of exercise
- Smoking
- Stress
- Too much alcohol

Precautions to reduce the risk of heart disease

- **Lifestyle changes:** Take enough exercise, avoid smoking, reduce stress and avoid alcohol
- **Reducing fat** intake, especially saturated fat, as outlined below

Guidelines to reduce fat intake

- Avoid high-fat sauces such as cream or cheese sauces
- Avoid pastries and cakes
- Choose low-fat dairy products
- Choose low-fat unsaturated spreads
- Grill, steam, bake or microwave instead of frying food
- Eat lean meat, fish or poultry without the skin

Vegetarian diets

A vegetarian does not eat meat.
There are two types of vegetarians:

- **Lactovegetarians:** They do not eat meat, fish or poultry. They eat animal products such as eggs, milk and cheese
- **Vegans:** They do not eat meat, fish, poultry, eggs, milk or dairy products. They live on fruit, vegetables, cereals and nuts

Guidelines for a healthy lactovegetarian diet

- Eat a very wide variety of foods to get enough **protein**. Include pulses, nuts and meat substitutes, e.g. textured vegetable protein (TVP) and quorn
- Choose whole cereals and fortified cereals to get enough **iron** and **vitamin B group**
- Include a variety of fruit and vegetables to get enough **vitamin A** and **C**

- Lactovegetarians should include milk and dairy products to provide **calcium**. Vegans can get **calcium** from fortified soya milk and green leafy vegetables
- Read food labels to avoid animal products

Vegetarian dishes

- **Savoury main course dishes:** Vegetable pie, vegetarian chilli con carne, vegetable burgers
- **Sweet dishes:** Fruit salads, fruit tarts, carrot cake

Coeliac disease

- Coeliac disease is an **intolerance** to a **protein** substance called **gluten**
- **Gluten** is a substance found in **wheat**
- Therefore, foods containing gluten must be excluded from a coeliac diet

Foods to Avoid	Foods Allowed
Wheat, rye, oats, barley	Rice, corn, soya, buckwheat
Bread, cakes, biscuits, crackers, pasta, noodles and breakfast cereals containing wheat, rye, oats or barley	Gluten-free bread, cakes and biscuits and crackers, pasta, noodles and breakfast cereals
Flour made from wheat, rye, oats or barley	Gluten-free flour

Gluten-free foods

The gluten-free symbol is used on the label of foods which do not contain gluten.

Diabetes

- Diabetes is a condition which occurs when **the body does not produce enough insulin** OR when **the body cannot use the insulin it produces**
- **Insulin** is a hormone needed to control the level of glucose (sugar) in the blood
- **Type 1 diabetes (insulin dependent):** This occurs when insulin is not produced in the body. When there is not enough insulin, the body does not get the energy it needs from glucose. The glucose collects in the blood and then it is excreted in the urine. If there is too much or too little sugar in the blood, the diabetic feels unwell and could become unconscious
- **Type 2 diabetes (non-insulin dependent):** This occurs when the body cannot use the insulin it produces. It happens mainly in adults and it is linked to being overweight. It is controlled by weight loss and a strict diet

Dietary guidelines to control diabetes

- Reach and maintain the ideal weight
- Eat regularly and never miss a meal or snack
- Eat high-fibre carbohydrate foods
- Avoid foods high in sugar. Some artificial sweeteners may be used instead of sugar
- Exercise regularly to balance blood sugar levels

Sample exam question

Question

Obesity has become a major health hazard.
(a) Outline the causes of obesity.
(b) List four health problems associated with obesity.
(c) Suggest four healthy eating guidelines which should be followed to reduce the risk of obesity.
(d) Plan a set of menus for one day suitable for an adult who is obese.
(e) Explain the term *empty kilocalories*.

(2003, HL)

Your revision notes

1.4 Food safety and storage

●●●Learning Objectives

In this chapter you will learn to:
1 List the causes of food spoilage
2 Summarise the advantages and disadvantages of microorganisms
3 Explain how food becomes infected by bacteria
4 Identify four common food poisoning bacteria and describe how they contaminate foods
5 Summarise food hygiene guidelines
6 Describe how to store non-perishable, semi-perishable and perishable foods
7 Explain the star markings found on frozen foods
8 Identify food packaging materials

Causes of food spoilage

Food spoilage is caused by **enzymes** (chemicals which occur naturally in food and cause ripening and decay) and **microorganisms** such as **moulds, yeasts and bacteria**.

Moulds

These appear like whiskers or soft cotton wool on food.

Advantages	Disadvantages
● Moulds are used to make antibiotics, e.g. penicillin ● They are used to make blue cheeses, e.g. Cashel Blue, and soft cheeses, e.g. Camembert	● Moulds spoil the appearance and taste of food

Yeasts

Yeasts are larger than bacteria and grow on foods containing moisture and sugar, such as fruit, fruit juices and syrups.

Advantages	Disadvantages
● Yeasts are used in bread-making, brewing and wine-making and to produce vitamin supplements	● Yeasts affect the taste and texture of food

Bacteria (germs)

Bacteria are invisible to the naked eye. They are found everywhere – on our skin, in our bodies, in the air, in sinks and on worktops and on our clothes. In small amounts most bacteria are harmless. This is known as 'an acceptable level of contamination'.

> **Points to note**
>
> **Bacteria** is the plural of **bacterium**.

Advantages	Disadvantages
• Bacteria are used to make cheese, yoghurt and vinegar	• Bacteria can cause food spoilage, food poisoning and other diseases

The growth of microorganisms

Microorganisms, such as bacteria, need **food, warmth, moisture** and **time** to grow and multiply.

1 **Food:** Bacteria thrive on moist high-protein foods
2 **Warmth:** The ideal temperature for most bacteria is 30–45°C. Boiling kills most bacteria and cold temperatures slow down their growth. Freezing does not kill bacteria
3 **Moisture:** Bacteria thrive best in damp conditions and in moist foods
4 **Time:** When the correct conditions for growth are present, bacteria can double in number every 10 to 20 minutes

How food becomes infected by bacteria

Bacteria cannot move on their own. They must be carried by any one of the following:

- Different types of foods
- Dirty utensils and work surfaces
- Air
- Hands
- Cuts and sores
- Water
- Vermin (rats and mice)

Humans carry bacteria in the intestine, nose, mouth and on the hands, particularly if they do not wash them after using the toilet or handling pets.

Cross-contamination occurs when unaffected food becomes contaminated by bacteria from another food, e.g. when raw and cooked meats are placed on the same board.

Insects carry dirt and bacteria on their legs. When they land on food, they vomit and excrete on it as they eat.

Pets and vermin (rats and mice) also carry bacteria and should be kept out of the kitchen and away from food.

Kitchen cloths and dirty kitchen utensils provide a breeding ground for bacteria, particularly if used cloths are left in a warm kitchen.

Food poisoning

Food poisoning is an illness caused by eating food or drinking liquids which have been contaminated by large numbers of **pathogenic** (disease-causing) **bacteria.** The symptoms are stomach pains, nausea, diarrhoea and vomiting. Here are some of the most common food-poisoning bacteria:

Salmonella

This is present in the intestines of animals and humans. It is spread by flies and vermin and by poor standards of personal hygiene. It is essential that hands are washed after using the lavatory in order to avoid salmonella. Meat, poultry, eggs and shellfish may be contaminated.

Staphylococci

These bacteria are found in the nose, throat and skin and in cuts and boils. It is essential that food handlers cover any cuts and do not cough or sneeze over food to avoid the spread of staphylococci. Unpasteurised milk and cold meats may be affected.

Listeria

This may grow and multiply in chilled foods as it prefers lower temperatures than other bacteria. It may contaminate poultry, pâté, soft cheeses, coleslaw, pre-cooked chilled meals and chilled pre-packed salads. Pregnant women should avoid these foods as listeria may cause miscarriage.

E.coli

This is found in the intestines of animals and humans. High standards of hygiene and thorough cooking of foods are essential to prevent E-coli poisoning. Foods most at risk include undercooked minced beef and beef burgers, salami, unpasteurised milk, cheese and yoghurt.

Clostridium botulinum

This bacterium occurs in faulty cans of food. It causes a very serious form of food poisoning called botulism, which can be fatal. Avoid cans with defects or leaks and ensure that food is thoroughly cooked.

Food hygiene guidelines

Remember ...

... 6 points for each.

Food

1 Keep all foods cool, clean and covered
2 Store perishables in a cool place
3 Check expiry dates on perishables
4 Keep raw and cooked meats separate to avoid cross-contamination
5 Use separate chopping boards for raw and cooked foods
6 Cook eggs, meat, fish and poultry thoroughly to kill bacteria

Food handler

1 Maintain a high standard of personal hygiene
2 Wash hands **before** handling food and **after** handling rubbish, using a tissue, using the toilet or handling pets

3 Cover or tie back hair and wear a clean apron

4 Handle food as little as possible

5 Avoid touching face or hair while preparing food

6 Keep fingernails clean and short. No nail varnish!

The kitchen

1 The kitchen should be well-designed, with adequate lighting and ventilation

2 Ensure that a plentiful supply of hot water and cleaning materials are available

3 All work surfaces and equipment should be washed and disinfected regularly

4 Kitchen cloths should be changed and disinfected regularly

5 Keep kitchen bin covered. Empty daily and disinfect once a week

6 Disinfect sink and draining board regularly

Food storage

It is essential to store food properly to ensure that it remains in prime condition for as long as possible.

Proper storage:

- Protects the food from flies and dust
- Prolongs its shelf life
- Makes finding the food easier in the kitchen
- Ensures that the kitchen is clean and well organised

Points to note

The **shelf life** of a food is the length of time it remains safe and fit to be eaten.

Guidelines for storage

1 Store foods correctly according to their type:

(a) **Non-perishables**, e.g. dry, bottled and tinned foods – Store in a cupboard in their own or in airtight containers.

(b) **Semi-perishables**, e.g. bread, cakes, fresh fruit and vegetables – Store breads and cakes in a breadbin or tin. Fruit and vegetables may be stored in a rack or basket. Some semi-perishables, such as salad vegetables, may be stored in the refrigerator.

(c) **Perishables**, e.g. eggs, milk, cream, fresh meat, frozen or fresh 'ready to cook' meals, etc. – These have the shortest shelf life and must be used within 3 or 4 days. Store in the refrigerator at 4°C.

(d) **Frozen food** – Store in the freezer at −18°C.

2 Note the 'best before' and 'use by' dates on perishables

3 Use up older foods before opening new ones

4 Store foods away from cleaning agents

5 Keep cupboards and storage containers clean to prevent contamination by bacteria

6 Once packages are opened, store dry foods like rice and pasta in airtight containers to prevent them becoming stale or infested by insects

7 Never refreeze thawed frozen food

Star Markings on Frozen Foods and Freezers	
*	Keeps for 1 week at −6°C
* *	Keeps for 1 month at −12°C
* * *	Keeps for 3 months at −18°C
* * * *	Keeps for up to 1 year at −18°C

Packaging materials

Many disposable and reusable materials are available for storing foods.

- **Disposable** packaging, such as **greaseproof paper** and **cling film**, should be used only once, as they cannot be cleaned thoroughly after use

- **Plastic, china, glass** and **tin** containers may be **reusable**. Some have sealable lids to prevent food drying out

Sample exam question

Question

(a) Outline the conditions that favour the growth of microorganisms.
(b) (i) Name one food-poisoning bacterium.
    (ii) Give two possible sources of this bacterium.
(c) List three symptoms of food poisoning.

(2005, HL)

Your revision notes

1.5 Meal planning and food presentation

●●● Learning Objectives

In this chapter you will learn to:
1. Recommend guidelines for planning meals
2. Differentiate between 'table d'hôte' and 'à la carte' menus
3. Differentiate between a garnish and a decoration
4. Suggest suitable garnishes and decorations for different foods
5. Compile a set of guidelines for table setting

Guidelines for planning meals

When planning meals, you should consider the following points:
1. Nutrition
2. Cost
3. Time
4. Skill
5. Equipment available
6. Personal preferences and dietary restrictions
7. Time of year and seasonal availability
8. Variety
9. The occasion

Remember ...

... 9 points.

Menus

A menu is a list of all the dishes served at a meal. There are two types of menus commonly found in restaurants: table d'hôte and à la carte.

Guidelines for writing your own menus

When writing menus for family meals or cookery assignments, there is no need to offer a choice within courses. Use a blank card or a folded sheet of stiff paper.

Follow these guidelines:
- Write dishes in the centre of the card
- List courses in the order in which they will be eaten – starter, main course, dessert
- Be very specific about the type, cut and cooking method of meat used
- Mention accompaniments, e.g. sauces
- Avoid using words like 'and' or 'served with'

Table d'hôte	À la carte
• A set menu with two to five courses • Limited choice within each course • Usually less expensive than à la carte	• A long list of dishes, each priced separately • Great variety • Usually more expensive than table d'hôte

Sample menus

Breakfast menus

Frozen berry smoothie

***

Muesli
Milk

***

Wholemeal bread
Tea/coffee

Orange juice

***

Porridge
Milk

***

Grilled sausages and bacon
Poached egg on toast

***

Croissants, toast
Coffee/hot chocolate

Light lunch or supper menus

Spanish tortilla
Green salad
Garlic bread

***

Apple pie
Ice cream

Cheese and mushroom omelette
Rocket salad
Baked potato

***

Baked bananas

Lunch or dinner menus

Florida cocktail

***

Chicken and cashew nut stir-fry
Egg noodles

***

Rhubarb and strawberry crumble

Custard sauce

French onion soup

***

Roast chicken
Bread sauce
Baked potatoes
Boiled carrots, peas

***

Baked Alaska

Food presentation

When food is presented and served attractively it stimulates the appetite and encourages us to eat.

- All serving dishes and tableware should be spotlessly clean and any spillages or splashes should be wiped from plates before serving the food
- All hot dishes should be served piping hot on hot plates. Cold dishes should be served on cold plates
- Ensure that the table is properly set with all the requirements before the meal is served
- A **garnish** or **decoration** will improve the appearance of the dish if properly chosen and tastefully used

Points to note

A **garnish** is used with savoury foods.
A **decoration** is used on sweet foods.

Garnishes

Here are some suggestions for **garnishing savoury dishes/foods:**

- **Soup:** Chopped parsley, cream, croutons
- **Fish dishes:** Lemon wedges or twists, sprig or chopped parsley, tomato basket, sauce (either with the fish, on the side of the plate or in a sauceboat)
- **Meat and salad dishes:** Sprigs of fresh herbs, chopped herbs, julienne vegetables, tomato rose, sliced cucumber or tomato, edible flowers, e.g. chive or nasturtium

Decorations

Here are some suggestions for **decorating sweet foods:**

- **Pastry dishes:** Pastry leaves or other shapes, sieved icing sugar or caster sugar
- **Cakes and desserts:** Piped cream decorations, fruit decorations, e.g. glacé cherries or strawberry fans, feathered glacé icing, chopped nuts, chocolate (grated, curls or leaves), 'hundreds and thousands', angelica

Table setting

Table settings may vary according to the occasion, the type of meal being served and the needs of the diners. Here are some guidelines:

- All cutlery should be **clean** and polished and glassware should be sparkling
- Cutlery is placed in **order of use**, i.e. cutlery used first is placed on the outside and diners work from the outside inwards
- Tablemats or tablecloths should be **spotless**
- Ensure **condiment containers** (for salt, pepper, mustard, etc.) are clean and filled
- **Napkins** may be rolled or folded and placed on side plate
- Choose a low **centrepiece** so that the diners can see one another across the table
- Place **iced water** on the table just before the guests are seated
- When serving a guest, **serve** from the left and take away from the right

Sample exam questions

Question

1 (a) Plan and set out a suitable menu for a picnic lunch for you and
      your friends.
  (b) Give two reasons for your choice of food and drink items.
  (c) Make a list of the equipment you would pack.
  (d) State how you would keep the food cool on a warm day.

(1998, OL)

2 Plan and set out a menu for a two-course main meal for yourself and three friends
  that can be prepared and served in 1 hour. Evaluate the nutritive value of the meal.

(1998, HL)

1.6 Starting to cook

●●●**Learning Objectives**

In this chapter you will learn to:
1 Summarise guidelines for safety, efficiency and hygiene when cooking
2 Recommend how to modify recipes in line with healthy eating guidelines
3 Describe how to use and care for food preparation equipment
4 Compile a list of guidelines for choosing appliances
5 List the reasons why food is cooked
6 List the effects of cooking on food
7 Describe three methods of heat transfer
8 Evaluate the various cooking methods

Starting to cook

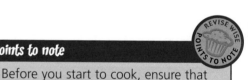

Points to note

Before you start to cook, ensure that **you**, your **work area** and your **equipment** are **clean**!

BEFORE

- Wear clean, protective **clothing**
- Tie back or cover **hair**
- Wash **hands** before touching food and after contact with any of the following: toilet, rubbish bin, animals, handkerchief, soil or raw meat
- Cover any **cuts**
- Ensure all **equipment, work surfaces, sinks and floor** are clean
- Having selected a recipe, collect all the necessary **ingredients**
- Collect all the **equipment** required
- **Weigh and measure** ingredients and arrange on plates or bowls on the table
- Pre-heat **oven** if necessary
- **Prepare** tins/dishes

DURING

- Follow your **recipe** step-by-step. **Clear away** peelings, skins or egg shells as you go along
- Keep the table **clean** and free of clutter. Wipe up spills immediately
- **Wash up** as you go along, if possible
- Keep **perishables** in the fridge until required
- Do not lick **fingers** when preparing food
- Avoid touching your **hair** or **face**
- Do not place the **tasting spoon** in food after use
- Avoid **wasting** food
- Use **oven gloves** when handling hot utensils
- Take care when using **sharp knives**
- Turn **saucepan handles** in, away from the edge of the cooker

AFTER

- **Clean up** properly after you have finished
- **Stack** dirty utensils to one side of sink, wash and stack washed utensils on the draining board
- Ensure all equipment is dried properly and **replaced** correctly

Recipes

A **recipe** is a set of instructions for making something from a given list of ingredients.

Weighing and measuring

In order to get good results when cooking, you must know how to weigh and measure ingredients accurately.

- Dry, solid foods are weighed in **grams (g)** and **kilograms (kg)**
- Liquid foods are measured in **millilitres (ml)** and **litres (l)**
- A **measuring jug** is used to **measure liquids** such as milk, water and stock
- A **weighing scale** is used to weigh dry foods such as flour and sugar
- **Spoons** are also used to measure dry or liquid ingredients

Points to note

1 teaspoon (**1 tsp**) = 5ml or 5g
1 dessertspoon (**1 dessertsp**) = 10ml or 10g
1 tablespoon (**1 tbsp**) = 15ml or 15g
(all level spoonfuls)

Temperature

- When a dish is to be cooked in the **oven**, it is important that the oven is set to the **correct temperature** and that the shelves are in the **correct position**
- The oven must be **pre-heated** so that it has reached the correct temperature by the time the dish is ready to cook. Allow 10–15 minutes to pre-heat

Recipe modification

Recipes may be **modified** (changed) for the following reasons:

- To make the dishes **healthier** (by adapting them to the healthy eating guidelines)
- To change the **size** of the dish
- To introduce **variety**
- To **substitute** for missing ingredients

Here are some suggestions for modifying recipes to suit healthy eating guidelines.

Remember ...

... 4 points for each.

To reduce sugar:
1 Toss fruit salad in unsweetened fruit juice
2 Use dried fruit, such as dates, sultanas or raisins, in fruit pies and crumbles to replace sugar and add fibre
3 Use artificial sweeteners where possible
4 Eliminate sugar from scones and breads

To reduce fat:
1 Remove visible fat on meat
2 Dry-fry meat in a non-stick pan (minced meat, rashers) and pour off excess fat
3 Use skimmed or low-fat milk when making sauces
4 Serve low-fat plain yoghurt instead of cream

To reduce salt:
1 Reduce or eliminate salt from recipes
2 Flavour foods with pepper, herbs and spices instead of salt
3 Use low-sodium salt
4 Avoid using commercial stock cubes

To increase fibre:
1 Leave skins on fruit, if possible, when used in fruit salads or other recipes
2 Use dried fruits for desserts
3 Substitute wholemeal pasta and rice for the white variety
4 Add pulse vegetables to savoury dishes, e.g. casseroles and chilli

Food preparation equipment

Equipment for food preparation can be divided into three main groups:
1 Small equipment (utensils)
2 Small appliances
3 Large appliances

Small equipment

This includes knives, forks, spoons, vegetable peelers, mashers, balloon whisks, flour dredgers, pastry brushes, palette knives, spatulas and graters. These are called **utensils**.

Utensil	Use
Spatula	To scrape food from bowls etc.
Balloon whisk	To whisk or beat ingredients
Flour dredger	To sprinkle flour
Pastry brush	To brush on water, egg wash or oil
Palette knife	To mix pastry
Grater	To grate cheese or fruit zest
Masher	To mash vegetables
Peeler	To peel fruit and vegetables

Kitchen utensils are made from a variety of different materials and need to be cared for accordingly.

Material	Care and Cleaning	Utensils
Plastic	Wash in hot soapy water. Rinse and dry. Keep away from direct heat	Fish slice, spatula, flour dredger, masher, chopping board
Wood	Wash in warm soapy water, scrubbing with the grain. Rinse and dry thoroughly before storing. Keep away from direct heat, while damp, as they may warp	Rolling pin, wooden spoons and spatulas, pastry brush, chopping board
Glass and delph	Wash in hot soapy water. Rinse and dry. Never place on a cold surface while hot or they may crack	Measuring jug, plates, bowls, pyrex plates and dishes
Metals (aluminium, tin, stainless steel)	Wash in hot soapy water. Rinse and dry very well before storing or they may rust. Never use abrasives or sharp utensils on non-stick pans. Store saucepans without lids to allow circulation of air	Saucepans, pans, woks, baking tins, grater, sieve, balloon whisk

Small appliances

These are small, portable, electrical items which save time and energy when preparing food, e.g. food mixer, food processor, juice extractor and liquidiser.

Appliance	Use
Food mixer	To cream, whisk or beat ingredients
Food processor	To blend, chop, grate or slice ingredients
Juice extractor	To squeeze fruit juice
Liquidiser	To purée, chop or blend ingredients

When using small appliances:

- Always follow the **manufacturer's instructions**
- When **cleaning**, never immerse the motor in water. Wipe over with a damp cloth
- To clean liquidisers and food processors, **half-fill** with hot soapy water and switch on. Take apart, rinse and dry well
- **Store** with lids off to allow circulation of air

Large appliances

These are large pieces of equipment which are not usually moved. When **choosing** an appliance, consider the following:

1 **Cost:** How much does it cost to buy and run?
2 **Safety:** Is it safe to use? Does it have an electrical safety mark?
3 **Suitability:** Are its size and specifications suitable for the needs of the user?
4 **Use and maintenance:** How easy is it to use and clean after use?

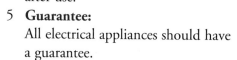

Remember …

… 6 points.

5 **Guarantee:** All electrical appliances should have a guarantee.
6 **After-sales service:** Can it be serviced locally?

Cooking food

Reasons for cooking food

- Harmful bacteria on food are killed by cooking. This makes the food safer to eat
- Cooking develops the flavour and appearance of many foods
- Cooking makes foods easier to digest. However, overcooking makes foods indigestible
- Cooking preserves food so that it lasts longer
- Certain methods of cooking make foods more attractive, e.g. roast meats, toasted savoury dishes

Effects of cooking on food

Cooking can have the following effects on food:

- Fat melts
- Colour changes
- Food forms a skin
- Food becomes solid
- Food softens and absorbs water
- Food softens and breaks up
- Nutrients are lost

Effects of overcooking on food

- Foods, e.g. cheese, become indigestible
- Increased loss of vitamins and minerals
- Colour, flavour and texture are damaged

Methods of heat transfer in cooking

Heat travels to food in the following ways:

- Conduction
- Convection
- Radiation

Conduction

Heat travels through something **solid**, e.g. a metal. This occurs when the heat travels from a hot saucepan or frying pan into the food.

Convection

Heat travels with **air or liquid which is moving**, e.g. water or oil. This happens in a fan oven where the air is moving around the food. It also occurs when food is being boiled because the liquid is moving around the food.

Radiation

Heat travels to food in **rays** in the same way that it travels to earth from the sun. Radiation occurs when food is grilled. The food does not touch the grill but the heat reaches the food.

Cooking methods

Food can be cooked:

- **Using fat**, such as roasting and frying
- Using **moist methods**, such as boiling, poaching, stewing, casseroling, steaming and pressure cooking
- Using **dry methods**, such as baking and grilling
- Using a **microwave**

Reasons for coating food before cooking

Foods are coated:

- To protect them from the hot fat during frying
- To improve the texture, e.g. to make it crispy
- To improve the flavour
- To prevent food from breaking up, e.g. fish coated in batter

Advantages and disadvantages of cooking methods

Cooking Methods	Advantages	Disadvantages
Using fat or oil Roasting Frying	• Excellent flavour and texture • Frying is quick	• High in fat • Fried food must be served immediately
Moist methods Boiling Poaching Stewing Casseroling Steaming Pressure cooking	• Low in fat • Tougher cuts of meat can be boiled or stewed	• Vitamins and minerals dissolve into the cooking liquid when boiling • Flavour may be bland when boiling and steaming
Dry methods Baking Grilling	• Low in fat • Little loss of nutrients	• Grilling is not suitable for tough cuts of meat • Food may become dry

Cooking methods using fat or oil

Cooking Method	Description	Suitable Foods
Roasting	Cooking food in an oven using hot fat or oil	Vegetables Meat Poultry
Frying (deep frying, shallow frying, stir-frying)	Cooking food in hot fat or oil in a frying pan or deep fat fryer	Eggs Vegetables Tender cuts of meat Fish Chips

Moist methods of cooking

Cooking Method	Description	Suitable Foods
Boiling	Cooking food in rapidly bubbling water in a saucepan	Pasta Rice Meat Vegetables
Poaching	Cooking food in water which is barely bubbling	Eggs Fruit Fish
Stewing/Casseroling	Cooking food slowly in a little liquid in a covered container	Meat Poultry Fish Vegetables
Steaming	Cooking food in steam rising from boiling water	Fish Vegetables
Pressure cooking	Cooking food under pressure in a heavy saucepan with a special lid	Puddings Meat Vegetables Fruit for jam making

Dry methods of cooking

Cooking Method	Description	Suitable Foods
Baking	Baking is cooking food in dry heat in an oven	Potatoes Fruits Breads Cakes Tarts
Grilling	Cooking food by rays of heat in a hot grill	Tender cuts of meat Fish Vegetables Fruit

Microwave cooking

Cooking Method	Description	Suitable Foods
Microwave cooking	Microwaves cause the particles of food to vibrate. This causes heat to build up inside the food. The heat then travels through the food by conduction	Cooks most foods Thaws frozen food Reheats cooked foods

Accompaniments

An accompaniment is a food which is **served with a dish**, e.g. a sauce.

Reasons for serving accompaniments

- They improve the flavour
- They provide a variety of textures
- They can offset richness, e.g. apple sauce reduces the richness of roast pork
- Some accompaniments, such as mint sauce with lamb, are traditional

Sample exam question

Question

(a) List four guidelines which should be followed to ensure safe food preparation.

(b) Give three reasons why food is cooked.

(c) Name one cooking method which involves each of the following:
  (i) Moist cooking
  (ii) Dry cooking
  (iii) Cooking using oil or fat

(d) Give three effects of cooking on food.

(e) Explain why some foods are coated before cooking.

(2003, OL)

1.7 Foods

●●●Learning Objectives

In this chapter you will learn to:
1. Design menus for breakfast and packed meals
2. Summarise the classification, nutritive value, structure, types, dietary uses, effects of heat/cooking, processing and storage of the following foods: soups and sauces, meat, poultry and fish, eggs, milk and dairy foods, fruit and vegetables, cereals
3. List guidelines for home baking and explain how a raising agent works
4. Describe methods of cake making and compile a set of guidelines for pastry making

Breakfast

Breakfast is the first and most important meal of the day. It is the fuel that gets you going so that you can face the day ahead and all its challenges.

For a healthy breakfast, try to include a variety of foods from all the food groups, if possible.

Cereal and potato group:
- Cereals: Porridge, muesli, cornflakes, Weetabix, All-Bran, Shredded Wheat, Fruit and Fibre, granola
- Breads: Wholemeal and white, toast, scones (white or brown), muffins, croissants, bagels
- Pancakes, crêpes and blinis

Fruit and vegetable group:
- Fruit juices, e.g. orange, grapefruit, apple, pear
- Fruit smoothies

- Stewed dried fruits, e.g. prunes, apricots
- Whole or half fruits, e.g. orange, grapefruit, banana
- Fruit segments or salads, e.g. orange, pineapple, mandarin

Milk group:
- Hot or cold milk with cereals
- Yoghurts, yoghurt drinks and yoghurt smoothies
- Cheeses
- Glass of milk or hot chocolate

Meat group:
- Eggs (boiled, poached, fried, scrambled, omelettes)
- Grilled rashers, sausages, black and white pudding
- Grilled kippers
- Kedgeree

Here are some examples of breakfast menus.

Strawberry and orange smoothie

***

Porridge
Honey

***

Croissants
Coffee

Freshly squeezed orange juice

***

Bran flakes
Milk

***

Grilled sausages and bacon
Scrambled eggs on toast

***

Brown soda bread, toast
Tea

Setting a breakfast tray

- Collect all the necessary equipment for a single place setting
- Ensure that all glassware and cutlery is sparkling
- Use small dishes and jugs for butter, marmalade, sugar and milk
- Include a mini floral arrangement to make it look attractive
- Set tray as shown opposite

Packed meals

A balanced packed lunch should include foods from the four food groups. Here are some suggestions:

Cereal and potato group:
- White or wholemeal bread, pitta bread, rolls, baps, crackers, scones, croissants, panini, tortilla wraps
- Muffins
- Barm brack
- Potato salad
- Spanish tortilla
- Cold pasta or rice salads
- Popcorn

Fruit and vegetable group:
- Fresh fruit, e.g. apples, oranges, bananas, kiwis
- Fruit juices and smoothies
- Fruit or vegetable salads
- Dried fruit
- Raw vegetable sticks, e.g. carrot and celery
- Vegetable soups
- Olives

Milk group:
- Milk, milkshakes, yoghurt, yoghurt drinks, smoothies, fromage frais
- Cheese
- Hot chocolate

Meat group:

- Hard-boiled eggs
- Cold sliced meats
- Nuts
- Tinned fish, e.g. tuna salad

- Chicken portions
- Sausage rolls
- Quiche
- Hummus

Here are some suggestions for packed lunch menus:

Slice of quiche
Potato salad
***
Strawberry smoothie
***
Mineral water

Tomato soup
***
Chicken salad pitta pocket
***
Blueberry muffin

Soups

Types of soup

Thin Soups	Thick Soups
• **Clear soups**, e.g. consommé • **Broths**, such as chicken broth, contain finely chopped meat or vegetables and an ingredient containing starch, e.g. pearl barley or pasta	• **Purée:** A soup which is thickened by liquidising after it has been cooked • **Thickened soups:** Starchy foods, such as flour, cornflour or roux, are used to thicken the soup

Stock

Points to note

Stock is water in which meat, fish or vegetables have been cooked.

Advantages of home-cooked stock are:

- It produces a fresh, wholesome flavour
- It is much lower in salt than commercial stock cubes
- It does not contain the additives commonly used in commercial stock cubes such as flavour enhancers (see flavour enhancers, p.67)

Characteristics of good soup

Soup should:

- Be well flavoured
- Have the right consistency, i.e. either thick or thin, and it should not have lumps
- Not be greasy
- Be served very hot

Garnishes for soup

- Herbs
- Croutons
- Cream

Convenience soups

- Dried soups
- Canned soups
- Cartons with long shelf life
- Chilled soups in containers

Advantages of Convenience Soups	Disadvantages of Convenience Soups
• Convenient to prepare • Useful in emergencies • Can be cheaper than the fresh variety, e.g. asparagus soup • Add variety to the diet	• Can contain excess salt • Can contain flavour enhancers such as monosodium glutamate • Chilled soups can be expensive • Inferior flavour, texture and food value when compared to freshly prepared soup

Sample exam question

Question

The following is a recipe for fresh vegetable soup.

Fresh Vegetable Soup
Ingredients

1 medium onion	1 litre stock
2 carrots	1 tbsp oil
2 potatoes	Pinch of salt
1 leek	Black pepper
50g peas	Herbs

(a) Name one root vegetable and one pulse vegetable used in this recipe.
Root vegetable _____
Pulse vegetable _____

(b) Suggest two garnishes suitable for this soup.

(c) Plan and set out a three-course dinner menu to include the vegetable soup.

(d) Give three reasons why vegetables are important in our diet.

(e) List three points to guide you when buying and storing fresh vegetables.

MENU

_____

_____

_____

_____

_____

_____

_____

_____

(2000, OL)

43

Sauces

Reasons for serving sauces with food

- Sauces add **flavour** to food
- They provide contrast to the **texture** of food
- They increase the **food value** of food (depending on the ingredients)
- They **moisten** foods
- They **offset the richness** in food, such as apple sauce with roast pork

Types of sauces

- **Egg-based** sauces, e.g. custard sauce
- **Fruit** sauces, e.g. cranberry sauce
- **Roux-based** sauces, e.g. cheese sauce
- **Cold** sauces, e.g. salad dressings

Convenience sauces

Advantages	Disadvantages
• Reduce preparation time • Useful for people with poor cooking skills • Wide variety available	• Can have high sugar content • Can have high salt content • May contain additives

- **Other sauces** include butterscotch sauce and chocolate sauces

Roux

- A roux is a mixture of equal quantities of fat and flour which are cooked together until smooth
- It is used for thickening sauces
- The consistency of roux-based sauces depends on the amount of liquid added
- Milk is used in white sauces and stock is used in dark sauces

Variations of white sauce

- Mushroom sauce
- Cheese sauce
- Parsley sauce

Sample exam question

Question

The following is a recipe for homemade cheese sauce.

Homemade Cheese Sauce Ingredients	
25g margarine	50g grated cheddar cheese
25g flour	$\frac{1}{4}$ teasp mustard
500ml milk	salt, pepper

(a) Based on the ingredients listed above:
  (i) evaluate the nutritive value of the homemade cheese sauce;
  (ii) identify the ingredients which are combined to form a roux.

(b) Name three dishes in which cheese sauce forms part of the main ingredients.

(c) Give four reasons why sauces may be used to accompany food.

(d) Suggest a different sauce which is traditionally served with each of the following roast meats:
  (i) turkey (ii) lamb (iii) pork

(e) Give two advantages and and two disadvantages of using convenience sauces.

(2003, HL)

Meat

Meat is the flesh of animals and birds. Meat also includes **edible offal**, which is the edible internal organs of animals, such as liver and kidney.

Nutritive value

- **Protein:** Meat is an excellent source of high biological value protein
- **Fat:** Meat contains saturated fat, both visible and invisible
- **Vitamins:** Meat contains B group vitamins
- **Minerals:** Meat is an excellent source of iron. It also contains calcium and phosphorus
- **Water:** Meat contains about 60 per cent water
- Meat does not contain **carbohydrate** and therefore it is served with foods containing carbohydrate, such as potatoes, pasta and bread

Composition of red meat

Protein	Fat	Carbohydrate
20–25%	20%	0%

Vitamins	Minerals	Water
B group	Iron Calcium Phosphorus	60%

Structure of meat

Meat is made up of long fibres. These fibres are held together in bundles by connective tissue.

Toughness in meat

Toughness in meat is caused by:
- **Age:** Older animals have tougher meat
- **Activity:** Meat from active parts of the animal, such as the leg, is tough. Meat from the back is tender

Tenderising meat

- **Hang** meat to allow enzymes to tenderise it
- **Pound** the meat with a steak hammer to break the fibres
- **Mince** or cut into small pieces
- Use **moist methods** of cooking such as stewing
- **Marinate** the meat before cooking, i.e. soak in a mixture of oil, vinegar and herbs and other flavouring ingredients
- Use **chemical tenderisers** such as papain

Buying meat

- Buy meat in a hygienic shop
- Meat should be firm, elastic and slightly moist
- It should not smell
- Check the expiry date on pre-packed meat
- Choose a suitable cut of meat for the dish you intend to cook

Points to note

Cheaper cuts of meat are just as nutritious as the more expensive cuts.

Storing meat

- **Separate raw meat from ready-to-eat foods to prevent cross-contamination**
- Fresh meat should be eaten within two days of purchase
- Remove wrapping from meat and place meat on a dish. Cover loosely to allow circulation of air

Marino Branch
Brainse Marglann Mhuirine
Tel: 8336297

- Store meat in a refrigerator or else freeze it
- Do not refreeze thawed meats
- Store meat low down in the fridge and use a dish large enough to prevent juices dripping onto other food
- Pre-packed meat should be used before the expiry date
- Cooked meat should be cooled quickly. It should be covered and stored in a refrigerator. Use within two days

Reasons for cooking meat

- Bacteria are destroyed which makes meat safer to eat
- Cooking improves the flavour
- Cooking improves the appearance of meat

Preparation of meat for cooking

- Defrost frozen meat thoroughly before cooking
- Remove meat from the refrigerator at least 1 hour before cooking
- Trim away visible fat. Wipe with kitchen paper
- Weigh meat to calculate the cooking time
- Choose a suitable cooking method for the cut of meat

Effects of cooking on meat

- Microorganisms are destroyed
- Protein coagulates on the surface, which seals in the juices
- The fat melts
- B group vitamins and some amino acids are destroyed
- The meat shrinks
- The flavour is improved
- The colour changes from red to brown

Using leftover meat

- Cover leftover meat, let it cool and place it in a refrigerator
- Separate cooked meat from raw meat in the refrigerator
- Use leftover meat within two days
- When reheating in a sauce, bring to the boil quickly and simmer until the food is thoroughly heated. Serve immediately
- Do not reheat food twice

Meat products

- Sausages
- Black and white pudding
- Burgers
- Pâté
- Cooked meats such as corned beef

Cooking Methods for Tender Cuts of Meat	Cooking Methods for Tough Cuts of Meat
Grilling	Stewing
Frying	Casseroling
Roasting	Boiling
Stir-frying	Pressure cooking
	Braising

Meat substitutes

Examples	Products
• Textured vegetable protein (TVP) • Quorn	• Burgers • Meat pies • Chicken-based meals • Sausages • Meat sauces

Meat substitutes have become **more popular** in recent years because:
- They are cheaper than meat
- They have a similar food value to meat but they contain less fat and more fibre
- They make meat go further when combined with it
- There is no waste
- They are suitable for vegetarians
- They have a long shelf life compared to meat

Poultry

Poultry is the flesh of specially reared domestic birds.

Guidelines to avoid food poisoning

Buying and preparing fresh poultry
- Buy poultry in a hygienic shop
- Avoid poultry which has an unpleasant smell or is discoloured or bruised
- Fresh poultry should be covered and stored in a refrigerator
- Keep raw poultry away from ready-to-eat foods in order to avoid cross-contamination
- Use poultry within the expiry date

Buying and preparing frozen poultry
- Poultry should be frozen solid
- Packaging should be sealed
- Transfer frozen poultry to a freezer as soon as possible after purchase
- Thaw frozen poultry thoroughly before cooking
- Once thawed, do not refreeze

> **Points to note**
> **Free range poultry** is poultry which is allowed to wander freely in a natural environment.

> **Points to note**
> **Salmonella** is a food-poisoning bacterium which is associated with poultry.

Sample exam question

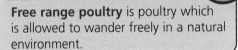

Question

(a) Give four reasons why meat should be included in the diet.
(b) What guidelines should be followed when (i) buying, (ii) storing and (iii) cooking minced meat?
(c) Name three meat products.
(d) Give one example of a meat substitute.
(e) Why have meat substitutes become popular in recent years?

(2002, HL)

Fish

Nutritive value

- **Protein:** Fish contains almost the same amount of high biological value protein as meat
- **Fat:** Polyunsaturated fat is found in oily fish. White fish does not contain fat
- **Vitamins:** Vitamin B in all fish, A and D in oily fish
- **Minerals:** Iron in oily fish and shellfish, calcium in the bones of tinned fish and iodine in all types of fish
- **Water:** Oily fish contains less water than white fish or shellfish
- Fish does not contain **carbohydrate** and therefore is often served with foods which do contain carbohydrate

Classification of fish

Fish is classified into three groups according to its food value and its shape:
- **White fish**, e.g. whiting, cod, plaice
- **Oily fish**, e.g. salmon, mackerel, herring
- **Shellfish**, e.g. mussels, prawns, crab

Composition of fish

Nutrient	White Fish	Oily Fish	Shellfish
Protein	17–20%	17–20%	17–20%
Fat	0%	13%	2.5%
Carbo-hydrate	0%	0%	0%
Vitamins	B group	A,D, B group	B group
Minerals	Iodine	Iodine	Iodine, Calcium
Water	70–80%	65%	72%

Buying fresh fish

- Fish should look fresh. The eyes should be bright and bulging. The gills should be bright red
- Markings should be bright and clear. For example, the red spots on plaice should be bright red
- Skin should be moist and unbroken
- Scales should not come off easily
- Fish should not smell 'fishy' but sea fish should have a slight sent of the sea
- Buy fish which is in season if possible because it is cheaper and has a better flavour

Buying frozen fish

- The packet should be frozen solid
- Fish must be used within the expiry date
- The packet should be sealed
- Place in the home freezer as soon as possible

Storing fresh fish

- Remove wrapping and rinse in cold water
- Place it on crushed ice and cover with more ice, if possible
- Cover to prevent the flavour from entering other foods
- Place in the refrigerator away from ready-to-eat foods
- Use within 24 hours

Storing frozen fish

- Store as soon as possible in a freezer
- Use within the expiry date
- Follow the manufacturer's instructions for thawing and cooking

Preparing fresh fish

1 If the skin is being left on, remove scales by scraping with a knife from tail to head and rinse
2 Cut off the head
3 Slit underside of fish and remove the gut. For flat fish, slit below the gill and remove the gut
4 Remove the fins and tail, using scissors
5 Remove any black membrane with salt
6 Rinse and dry, using kitchen paper

Effects of cooking/heat on fish

- Protein coagulates (sets)
- Fish becomes opaque
- Connective tissue dissolves and the fish breaks apart easily
- Minerals and vitamin B dissolve into the cooking liquid
- Microorganisms are destroyed

Sample exam question

Question

(a) Name one fish in each of the following groups.

White Fish	Oily Fish	Shellfish
(i)	(i)	(i)

(b) Give three reasons why fish should be included in the diet.
(c) Suggest three ways to encourage children to eat fish.
(d) Plan a packed lunch menu for a teenager which includes fish.
(e) List two guidelines which should be followed when storing fresh fish.

Packed Lunch Menu

_____

_____

_____

_____

_____

(2002, OL)

Eggs

Eggs are one of the most useful foods in the diet. They have a high nutritive value and many different uses.

Nutritive value

- The white contains high biological value **protein**
- The yolk contains **protein**, easily digested **fat, vitamins A, D** and **B, calcium, iron, sulphur** and **phosphorus**
- **Water** makes up 74 per cent of an egg
- Eggs **do not contain any carbohydrate**. They are usually served with starchy foods, e.g. scrambled egg on toast, to make up for this lack
- Eggs **lack vitamin C**

Structure of an egg

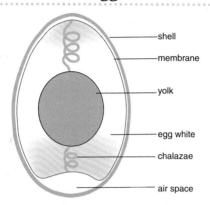

- shell
- membrane
- yolk
- egg white
- chalazae
- air space

Uses of eggs

1 **For eating on their own:** Scrambled, boiled, fried or poached
2 **Savoury dishes:** Quiche, omelette, pancakes
3 **Thickening:** Eggs are used to thicken mixtures like custards and cold desserts

Remember ...
... 10 points.

REVISE WISE REMEMBER

4 **Holding air:** Eggs trap and hold air when whisked, e.g. in sponges and meringues
5 **Binding:** Eggs are used to bind foods together, e.g. in fish cakes and hamburgers
6 **Glazing:** Beaten egg may be brushed on pastry, bread and scones to give an attractive finish
7 **To enrich:** Eggs can add extra protein and flavour to dishes like mashed potato or breads
8 **Garnishing:** Hard boiled, sliced or sieved
9 **Coating:** Foods, e.g. fish, may be coated in egg and breadcrumbs before frying
10 **Emulsions:** Eggs help to hold oil and vinegar together, e.g. in mayonnaise

Buying eggs

Every egg is individually stamped with a code which makes it fully traceable back to the farm where it was produced.

Look for the following information on the egg box:

- Number of eggs
- EU size: Small, medium and large
- EU egg class: Class is an indication of quality. Class A is the best quality
- Registration number of the packing station
- Name of the producer and/or packer
- 'Free range' will be printed on the box if the hens have had the freedom to roam in a natural environment. Their feed does not contain any additives or animal by-products

How to check for freshness

If a fresh egg is placed in salted water, it will sink to the bottom. A stale egg will float on or near the surface.

Storing eggs

- Store in a **cool place** such as a fridge
- **Do not wash** eggs as this removes their natural protective layer
- Store **away from strong-smelling foods** such as onions as the smell will be absorbed through the porous shell
- Store with the **pointed end down** so that the eggs will keep fresh for longer
- If storing separated eggs, place the yolks in a bowl and cover with water. Store whites in an airtight container. Store both in the fridge

Effects of cooking/heat on eggs

- Protein coagulates (sets). The egg white becomes cloudy and then white
- Eggs curdle if cooked at too high a temperature or for too long
- Overcooked eggs become hard and rubbery and are difficult to digest. Lightly cooked eggs are more digestible

Sample exam question

Question

(a) List four items of information shown on this egg box.

(b) What is meant by *free-range eggs?*

(c) Give three reasons why eggs are useful in the diet.

(d) Plan a balanced breakfast menu for a school-going child to include an egg dish.

(e) Name the food items in the menu that you have planned that come from each of the following food groups: Protein group; Fruit/Vegetable group; Milk group; Cereal/Bread group.

(2001, OL)

Milk and dairy foods

Milk is the most complete natural ready-made food there is. It is an essential part of a healthy diet.

Nutritive value of milk

Milk contains the following nutrients:

- **Protein** (high biological value) for growth
- **Fat** for heat, energy and insulation
- **Carbohydrate** for energy
- **Calcium and phosphorus** for bones and teeth
- **Vitamins A** and **D** for healthy skin, eyes and bones
- **Vitamin B** for healthy nerves and release of energy
- **Water**: 87 per cent of milk is water

Types of milk

- **Whole milk** or standard milk contains 3.5 per cent fat and is the most popular milk in Ireland
- **Low-fat milk** (semi-skimmed) milk contains 1.5 to 1.8 per cent fat. It is also called light milk
- **Skimmed milk** contains 0.1 to 0.3 per cent fat. It is not suitable for babies and young children as it lacks fat soluble vitamins
- **Fortified milk** is low-fat or skimmed milk with extra vitamins (A and D), folic acid and calcium added. Essential fatty acids may also be added

Points to note

Milk is **pasteurised** to kill harmful bacteria. The milk is heated to 72°C for 25 seconds and then cooled quickly. Whole milk is also **homogenised** to spread the cream evenly through the milk.

- **Buttermilk** is the remaining liquid after butter is made. 'Cultured' buttermilk has added bacteria to make it acid and sharp-tasting. It is used for baking
- **Evaporated milk** has some water removed before it is canned
- **Condensed milk** is similar to evaporated milk and has added sugar. Condensed and evaporated milks are used in sweet-making and in desserts
- **Dried milk** has all the water removed by evaporation
- **Ultra heat treated (UHT) milk** is heated to 132°C, then cooled and packed. It will keep for months without refrigeration. It is often called long-life milk
- **Soya milk** is made from soya beans and is used as a dairy milk substitute

Uses of milk in food preparation

Milk is an extremely versatile food. It has many different uses:

1 As a **drink** on its own or added to others, e.g. tea, milkshakes
2 In **baked foods**, e.g. bread, scones
3 In **breakfast cereals** (hot and cold)
4 In **sauces**, e.g. white sauce, parsley sauce, cheese sauce
5 In **desserts** and puddings, e.g. bread and butter pudding, rice pudding
6 In **savoury dishes**, e.g. quiche, pancakes
7 In **soups,** e.g. mushroom soup
8 As **milk products**, e.g. yoghurt, cheese

Remember ...
... 8 points.

Effects of cooking/heat on milk

- Bacteria are killed
- Flavour is changed
- Loss of vitamins B and C
- Protein coagulates (becomes solid) and forms a skin on the milk

Milk products

Cream, butter, yogurt and cheese are examples of milk products.

Cheese

Cheese-making is a natural and ancient method of preserving milk.

Nutritive value

Cheese contains the following nutrients:

- **Protein** (high biological value) for growth
- **Fat** for heat, energy and insulation. As this is saturated fat, eat in moderation
- **Lacks carbohydrate** and should be served with starchy foods
- **Calcium, phosphorus** and **magnesium** for bones and teeth
- **Vitamins A** and **D** for healthy skin, eyes, nerves and bones
- **Vitamin B** for healthy nerves and release of energy
- **Water**: low water content

Cheese production

1 Fresh milk is **pasteurised** to destroy harmful bacteria
2 **Bacteria** are added to sour the milk
3 **Rennet** is added to clot the milk
4 The milk now consists of **curd**, a solid part, and **whey**, a watery substance
5 The whey is removed and the curd is cut into pieces and **salted**
6 The cheese is **pressed** into moulds, lightly for soft cheeses and firmly for hard cheeses
7 Blocks of cheese are stored and allowed to **ripen** for between 3 and 12 months

Uses of cheese

Cheese may be used:

1 As a **snack**, with crackers or bread
2 In **salads and dressings**, e.g. blue cheese dressing
3 In savoury **dips** and fondues
4 In **savoury** dishes, e.g. pizza, quiche, lasagne
5 In **sauces**, e.g. cheese sauce

Remember ...

... 9 points.

6 In **biscuits, bread** and **scones**
7 In **cheeseboards** as an alternative to dessert
8 In **desserts**, e.g. cheesecake, tiramisu
9 As a **garnish**, sprinkled over pasta or au gratin dishes

Points to note

Au gratin describes food covered with grated cheese or breadcrumbs and browned in the oven or under the grill.

Types of cheese

- **Hard:** Cheddar, Emmenthal, Parmesan
- **Semi-soft:** Edam, Port Salut, Blarney
- **Soft:** Brie, Mozzarella, Cottage
- **Processed:** Cheese slices, e.g. Easi-singles, cheese spread, cheese strings
- **Blue-veined** cheeses: Irish Blue, Stilton, Gorgonzola. Cheeses are injected with a harmless blue mould
- **Farmhouse** cheeses: Gubbeen, Killorglin, Coolea. Locally produced cheeses, often made from unpasteurised milk.

Effects of cooking/heat on cheese

- Fat melts
- Protein coagulates (becomes solid) and shrinks
- Overcooking causes cheese to become stringy and indigestible

Storage of all dairy products

- Check the **use-by** and **best before** dates before buying any dairy products
- Store, covered, in a **cool, clean place** such as a refrigerator
- Keep milk **out of sunlight** which destroys vitamin B and sours it
- Pour milk into a **clean jug** when required
- Wrap cheese in **greaseproof paper** and cover with tin foil
- **Remove cheese from the fridge** about 1 hour before serving as the flavour of cheese is better when served at room temperature

Sample exam questions

Question

1 (a) Give three reasons for including cheese in the diet of an energetic child.
  (b) Name the main nutrient which is not present in cheese.
  (c) List two foods you could serve with cheese in order to present a balanced meal.
  (d) Suggest a way of making cheddar cheese more digestible.
  (e) Give three guidelines for the storage of cheese.

(1996, OL)

2 Milk is the most complete single natural food and it is very important in the diet.
  (a) List the nutrients found in milk.
  (b) Explain why milk is important in the diet.
  (c) Name three types of milk available in shops.
  (d) List four products made from milk.
  (e) Suggest four ways in which milk may be used in food preparation.
  (f) How should milk be stored?

(1999, HL)

Fruit and vegetables

Classification of vegetables

Vegetables are divided into four groups.

Greens	Roots	Pulses	Fruits
Broccoli	Carrot	Peas	Tomato
Spinach	Parsnip	Beans	Cucumber
Cabbage	Potato	Lentils	Pepper
Cauliflower	Onion		Courgette
Brussels sprouts	Swede		Aubergine
	Beetroot		Pumpkin

Composition of vegetables

Category	Protein	Fat	Carbohydrate	Vitamins	Minerals	Water
Greens	Trace	0%	2%	A, C	Calcium, iron	90–95%
Roots	Trace	0%	5–20%	A, C	Calcium, iron	75–90%
Pulses	2–7%	Trace	4–10%	A, C	Calcium, iron	75–90%
Fruits	Trace	0%	5–20%	A, C	Calcium, iron	80–90%

Nutritive value of vegetables

Nutrient	Vegetables
Protein	Peas, beans and lentils
Carbohydrate	**Sugar** is found in beetroot, carrots, parsnips and onions **Starch** is found in potatoes, pulses and root vegetables **Fibre** is found in all vegetables
Calcium	Green leafy vegetables, e.g. cabbage, and some root and pulse vegetables
Iron	Green leafy vegetables, e.g. spinach, and root vegetables
Trace elements	Pulse vegetables
Vitamin C	Fresh young vegetables
Vitamin A (carotene)	Carrots and green leafy vegetables
Vitamin B	Pulses
Water	All vegetables
Fat	Not found in most vegetables Small amount in pulses

Buying fresh fruit and vegetables

- Choose a shop or market with a quick turnover
- Buy fruit and vegetables in season
- Buy medium-sized young fruit and vegetables
- Choose fresh, brightly coloured vegetables
- Avoid bruised fruit and vegetables
- Buy in usable quantities
- Avoid pre-packed fruit and vegetables

Points to note

Organic vegetables are grown without the use of artificial fertiliser, pesticides or herbicides.

Points to note

At various times during the year, certain vegetables are plentiful and cheap, i.e. they are **in season**.

Storing fruit and vegetables

- Remove from packaging
- Store root vegetables on a rack in a cool, dark, dry, well-ventilated place
- Separate washed and unwashed vegetables
- Wash all vegetables before storing in a refrigerator
- Greens and fruit (except bananas) can be stored in a refrigerator
- Wash greens, dry in a salad spinner and place in a plastic bag
- Dried pulses should be stored in airtight jars
- Follow the manufacturer's instructions for storing frozen or other processed vegetables

Retaining nutrients in fruit and vegetables

Preparation

- Prepare just before cooking to avoid loss of nutrients
- Eat vegetables raw and unpeeled if possible
- Peel thinly to retain the fibre content
- Use a sharp knife to avoid damage to the vegetables
- Do not steep vegetables

Cooking vegetables

- Never use bread soda when cooking vegetables

- Cook for the shortest possible time. Cover with a lid and use the minimum amount of water to prevent loss of vitamins and minerals
- Do not reheat because vitamins are destroyed
- Use the cooking liquids in sauces to retain the vitamin and mineral content

Effects of cooking/heat on vegetables

- Vitamins and minerals dissolve into the cooking liquid
- Vitamin C is destroyed
- Fibre becomes soft
- Starch becomes more digestible
- Some colour, flavour and texture are lost depending on the cooking time and method

Classification of fruit

Citrus Fruit	Berries/Soft Fruit	Stone Fruit	Hard Fruit	Dried Fruit	Other
Oranges	Raspberries	Plums	Apples	Raisins	Grapes
Lemons	Blackberries	Apricots	Pears	Sultanas	Pineapples
Grapefruits	Strawberries	Peaches		Currants	Bananas
Limes	Gooseberries	Nectarines		Prunes	Melons
Satsumas	Blackcurrants	Cherries		Dates	Kiwis
Tangerines	Redcurrants	Avocados			Star fruits

Nutritive value of fresh fruit

Nutrient	Fruit
Carbohydrate	Fruit contains **sugar** and **fibre** **Fibre** is found particularly in the skin
Vitamin C	In fresh fruit, particularly in oranges and blackcurrants
Vitamin A	In orange, red, yellow and green fruit
Minerals	Dried fruit contains **calcium** and **iron**
Water	Fruit contains up to 95 per cent water
Protein	Bananas and dried fruit contain **very small amounts**
Fat	Only in avocados

Uses of fruit in the diet

- **Fresh** as a snack
- **Drinks:** Juices and in smoothies
- **Breakfast:** Fresh, with cereals or cooked
- **Packed lunches:** Fresh, dried, in yoghurts
- As **starters**, e.g. grapefruit, orange
- As **accompaniments** with a main course, e.g. lamb with apricots
- **Sauces:** Orange sauce
- **Salads:** Fresh fruit salad
- **Hot desserts:** Fruit tarts
- **Cold desserts:** Fruit flan
- **Baking:** Fruit cake, muffins
- **Preserves:** Chutneys, jams, etc.

Effects of processing/cooking on fruit

- Fruit becomes soft
- Vitamin C is reduced by up to 25 per cent or it may be destroyed completely
- Vitamin C and minerals dissolve into the cooking or canning liquid. This liquid should be used in sauces
- Microorganisms are destroyed
- Fibre becomes soft which makes fruit more digestible

Sample exam question

Question

Fruit forms an important part of a balanced diet.

Fruit	Protein	Carbohydrate	Minerals	Vitamins	Water
Fresh	Trace	5–20%	Calcium, iron	A, C	80–90%
Tinned	Trace	20–30%	Calcium, iron	A, C *reduced*	70–80%
Dried	Trace	50–60%	Calcium, iron *increased*	A	15–25%

(a) Using the nutritive information given in the table above:
   (i) Compare the food value of fresh fruit with tinned fruit **or** dried fruit;
   (ii) Give one function of each of the minerals listed in the table;
   (iii) What does 'trace' mean?
(b) Suggest two different uses for each of the three types of fruit listed in the table above.
(c) List the advantages of including fruit in the diet.
(d) Give three effects of processing on fruit.

(2004, HL)

Cereals and baking

Cereals are the **seeds or grains** of edible grass plants. They include **wheat, rice, rye, oats, barley** and **maize (corn)**.

Nutritive value

- Cereals contain low biological value **protein**
- A small amount of **fat** is present
- **Carbohydrate** is the main nutrient found in cereals. It is present in the form of **starch** and **fibre** (in unprocessed cereals). Refined cereal products have most of the fibre removed during processing
- The **vitamin B group** is present in unprocessed cereals
- **Iron, calcium** and **phosphorus** are also present
- The **water** content is low

Structure of a cereal grain

Here is what a grain of wheat would look like if cut in half and examined under a microscope.

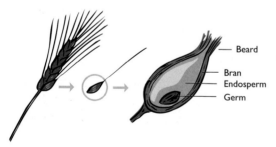

Beard

Bran
Endosperm
Germ

- The **bran** layer is the outer layer and provides fibre, iron and vitamin B. It is usually removed during the processing of cereals

- The **endosperm** is composed mainly of starch and a protein called gluten. Coeliacs cannot absorb gluten
- The **germ** contains protein, fat and vitamin B and is the most nutritious part of the grain

Processing of cereals

Cereals are usually processed in some way before we eat them. This makes them easier to chew and digest. The cereal grain is split up or parts of the grain (usually the bran and the germ) are removed, leaving only the endosperm.

- **Wholegrain** cereal products, e.g. wholemeal flour, wholemeal bread, brown rice and rolled oats, contain all or most of the cereal grain
- **Refined** cereal products, e.g. white flour, white bread, cornflour and white rice, are composed mainly of endosperm
- **Fortified** cereal products, e.g. white flour and breakfast cereals, have some of the vitamins and minerals which were removed during processing added back into the product

Effects of cooking on cereals

- Starch grains swell and burst, e.g. popcorn, pastry
- The grains absorb liquid, e.g. rice, or fat, e.g. pastry
- Starch becomes more digestible

Cereal products

Cereals are an extremely important source of food and may be used to manufacture many different products.

Wheat	Maize	Rye
• White and whole-meal flour • Bread • Pasta • Semolina • Weetabix and other breakfast cereals • Biscuits • Cakes • Noodles • Couscous	• Cornflakes and other breakfast cereals • Popcorn • Sweetcorn • Corn on the cob • Corn oil • Tortilla chips • Tacos	• Rye flour • Rye bread • Crispbread, e.g. Ryvita • Rye whiskey
Rice	**Barley**	**Oats**
• Brown and white rice • Ground rice • Rice paper • Rice flour • Rice Krispies	• Beer • Whiskey • Pearl barley	• Rolled oats • Oatmeal • Porridge • Muesli • Ready Brek and other breakfast cereals

Pasta

Pasta is made from durum wheat which is finely ground down into semolina and then mixed with water to form a dough. The addition of egg, spinach or tomatoes or the use of wholemeal semolina produces different colours.

Rice

The main types of rice are:

- **Long-grain or patna rice:** Used in savoury dishes and as an accompaniment to stews and curries
- **Medium-grain or risotto rice:** Used in risottos and dishes where the rice grains are moulded together
- **Short-grain rice:** Used for rice puddings and other sweet rice dishes

- **Brown rice:** Contains some of the bran layer. It has a nutty flavour and a chewy texture. Takes longer than white rice to cook
- **Basmati rice:** Long-grain rice with a distinct flavour and texture

Flour

Flour is made by grinding up cereals such as wheat, rice, oats, rye and maize. In Ireland, most flour is made from wheat.

Types of flour

- **Wholemeal flour:** Contains the whole wheat grain, with nothing added or taken away. Used for making wholemeal bread, scones, rolls and pastry

- **Brown flour:** Some of the bran and germ are removed during milling. Used for making brown bread and rolls and pastry
- **White flour:** All of the bran and germ are removed. It consists of starchy endosperm only. Used for making white bread and rolls, cakes, pastry, biscuits and for thickening soups and sauces
- **Self-raising flour:** Brown or white flour with a raising agent, e.g. baking powder, added. Uses as for white flour with the exception of pastry making and thickening
- **Strong flour:** Flour that is milled from spring wheat, which has a high gluten content. Used for making yeast bread and some pastries
- **Gluten-free flour:** The gluten is removed. Used to make bread, biscuits, etc. for coeliacs

Points to note

Gluten is a protein found in wheat. It makes the dough stretchy and elastic so that it rises well.

Home baking guidelines

1 Before starting to mix any ingredients, prepare **tins**, arrange **oven shelves** and **preheat oven** to the correct temperature at least 15 minutes before you start
2 Ensure all **ingredients** are fresh (check expiry dates)
3 **Weigh and measure** ingredients accurately according to recipe
4 Follow **recipe** carefully step by step
5 Take care when **adding liquid** to dry ingredients to ensure correct texture or consistency
6 **Knead lightly** and avoid overhandling pastry, bread and scone dough
7 **Time carefully** and avoid opening the oven door unnecessarily
8 Check to see if the cake is **cooked** using the appropriate method (see below)
9 **Cool** on a wire tray

How to test if a cake is cooked

- **Bread and scones**: Sound hollow when tapped underneath
- **Cakes** (madeira, all-in-one and fruit cakes): Warmed metal skewer comes out clean from the cake with no uncooked mixture clinging to it
- **Sponges** (whisked): Shrink in from the sides of the tin and spring back when pressed lightly with the fingers

Raising agents

A **raising agent** is a substance used to **produce a gas in a dough or batter**. When the gas is heated in the oven, it expands and rises which causes the dough to become light and well risen.
There are four types of raising agents:
1 Air
2 Bread soda
3 Baking powder
4 Yeast

Air

Air is a natural raising agent. It may be introduced into the mixture by:
- Sieving the flour
- Creaming ingredients
- Whisking ingredients
- Raising your hands high over the bowl when rubbing in fat

Air is used in pastry, batters, sponges and meringues.

Baking powder and bread soda

Baking powder and bread soda depend on a chemical reaction to produce the gas.

Baking Powder	Bread Soda
• A tin of **baking powder** contains a mixture of an acid and an alkali. These are activated when liquids such as milk, water or eggs are added. **Acid + Alkali + Liquid = CO_2** **Baking Powder + Milk/Water/Eggs = CO_2**	• **Bread soda** is an alkali. It must be combined with an acid and a liquid in order to produce CO_2. Buttermilk is both acid and liquid. **Alkali + Acid + Liquid = CO_2** **Bread Soda + Buttermilk = CO_2**
• Baking powder is used in all types of cakes, buns and biscuits.	• Bread soda is used in soda bread and scones, gingerbread and some cakes.

Yeast

Yeast is a microorganism which produces CO_2 in a dough. Yeast is used in commercially baked bread and homemade yeast bread, buns and some pastries, e.g. Danish pastries.

When the gas (O_2 or CO_2) has been produced in the dough, it is then put into the oven.

The heat of the oven causes the gas bubbles to expand.

The bubbles push upwards and make the dough rise.

The heat of the oven forms a crust on top and prevents any further rising.

Methods of making bread and cakes

Method	Procedure	Uses
Rubbing-in method	The fat is rubbed into the flour. The other dry ingredients are then added, followed by the liquid	Plain cakes, scones, pastry
Creaming method	The fat and sugar are creamed together, the eggs are beaten in and the flour is then folded into the mixture	Queen cakes, madeira cakes, rich fruit cakes
Whisking method	The eggs and sugar are whisked together until thick and creamy. The flour is then folded in very lightly	Sponge cakes, flans, Swiss rolls

Method	Procedure	Uses
All-in-one method	All the ingredients are placed in a bowl and beaten together. Soft tub margarine or block margarine at room temperature should be used	All-in-one madeira, chocolate or coffee cakes
Melting method	The ingredients which melt (fat, sugar, treacle and syrup) are heated and melted before being added to the dry ingredients	Gingerbread and boiled fruit cakes

Commercial cake mixes

Cake mixes consist of a mixture of flour, raising agent, fat, sugar and other additives. Dried milk or egg may also be included. They are made up by the addition of liquid ingredients (milk, water or eggs). Follow the instructions on the packet.

Advantages	Disadvantages
• Quick and easy • Labour saving • Give confidence to beginners • Useful in emergencies	• Expensive • Photos on package may be misleading • High in sugar and salt, low in fibre • May contain additives

Pastry

Pastry is a mixture of flour, fat and water which is made into a dough, then kneaded, shaped and baked. It may be used in sweet and savoury dishes.

Types of Pastry	Uses
Shortcrust	Sweet and savoury tarts, pies, flans, sausage rolls
Rich shortcrust	Sweet tarts, flans, pies
Cheese pastry	Cheese straws, biscuits, quiche, savoury flans
Wholemeal pastry	Savoury flans, quiches, pies, tarts
Flaky pastry, rough puff pastry, puff pastry	Pies, tarts, sausage rolls, mille feuille, vol au vents, mince pies
Choux pastry	Profiteroles, éclairs
Filo pastry	Spring rolls, savoury baskets, Baklava (a Greek dessert)

Guidelines for making pastry

1 Weigh ingredients accurately and use the correct proportions
2 Keep the ingredients and utensils as cool as possible
3 Add the water carefully. Use just enough to bind ingredients without becoming sticky
4 Mix with a knife and knead lightly on a floured board
5 Avoid overhandling
6 Roll pastry lightly and as little as possible
7 Avoid stretching pastry as it will shrink during baking
8 Allow pastry to relax in a refrigerator before baking
9 Bake in a hot oven so that the starch grains in the flour burst and absorb the fat

> **Remember ...**
> ... 9 points.

> **Points to note**
> To **bake blind** means to bake a pastry case without any filling.

Sample exam question

Question

Cereals are a staple food in many countries.
(a) Explain why cereals are important in the diet.
(b) List three different products made from each of the following cereals:
   (i) wheat (ii) rice.
(c) What is the difference between a *wholegrain* cereal product and a *refined* cereal product?
(d) Explain why some cereal products such as breakfast cereals may be fortified.
(e) Name three types of flour used in baking and suggest a different use for each.

(2001, HL)

1.8 Food processing

●●●**Learning Objectives**

In this chapter you will learn to:
1 Explain how food is preserved
2 Evaluate the various methods of food processing
3 Describe food labels
4 Name commonly used additives and state their functions
5 Evaluate the use of convenience foods

Reasons for food processing

- Food lasts longer
- Food requires less preparation than fresh food
- Food is easier to store
- Food is easier to transport
- Seasonal foods are available all year round

Points to note

Food processing means changing the natural state of a food.
Food preservation means treating food to make it last longer.

Food preservation

The **conditions** required for the growth of microorganisms are:
- **Food**
- **Warmth**
- **Moisture**
- **Time**
- **Oxygen:** Most microorganisms need oxygen from the air

If any of these conditions are removed, the food will last longer.

Methods of food preservation

- **Freezing:** Warmth and moisture are removed
- **Heat treatments** such as **canning** and **pasteurisation**: Microorganisms are destroyed
- **Drying**: Moisture is removed
- **Irradiation**: Destroys microorganisms
- **Preservatives** such as sugar, salt, vinegar and smoke: Microorganisms cannot live in a high concentration of these chemicals

Freezing

Freezing preserves food because it:
1 **Reduces the temperature of food** so that microorganisms are **inactivated** and cannot grow (−18°C to −30°C)
2 **Changes the water in food to ice**, and microorganisms cannot grow **without moisture** in the form of water

Points to note

One should **never refreeze** thawed food because once the food begins to thaw, there is a risk that microorganisms can multiply to dangerous levels which can lead to food poisoning.

Foods unsuitable for freezing

- Vegetables with a high water content such as cucumber as they loose texture
- Bananas and avocados as they blacken
- Milk, cream and mayonnaise as fat and water separate
- Whole eggs as they crack

Guidelines for packaging

- Packaging should be moisture proof and vapour proof
- Seal bags with wire ties or freezer tape
- Remove as much air as possible
- Allow headspace for liquids to expand
- Wrap sharp edges with foil to prevent tearing the packaging
- Label packages clearly

Types of freezer packaging

Examples of good freezer packaging are:
- **Bags:** Strong polythene freezer bags
- **Rigid containers:** Waxed cartons, plastic boxes and aluminium containers

Points to note

All vegetables should be **blanched** before freezing. Blanching involves **immersing food in boiling water for a short time** to kill enzymes which damage the colour, flavour and texture of food.

Buying frozen food

- Food should be frozen solid
- Check the expiry date
- Packaging should be intact and properly sealed
- Food should be stored below the load line in open freezers
- The temperature of shop freezers should be −18°C
- Buy frozen food from a reliable source

Storing frozen food

- Follow the instructions on the label
- Store in a deep freeze or in a star-marked refrigerator for no longer than the recommended time

Thawing frozen food

- Follow the instructions for thawing on the label
- Thaw food in a refrigerator or microwave for the recommended amount of time
- Many foods, such as vegetables and fish, are cooked from frozen
- Thaw food thoroughly, especially meat and poultry
- **Do not refreeze thawed food**

Canning

In the canning process **heat destroys microorganisms** and the food is kept in **airtight cans** to prevent any further contamination.

Buying canned food

- Do not buy damaged cans which are bulging, dented or rusting because the contents may contain microorganisms which cause food poisoning

- Read the label to check the contents. For example, fruit may be canned in syrup or fruit juice, and various sauces are used in canning meat and fish
- Check the expiry date

Drying

In the drying process, **heat removes the water** from food. This inactivates microorganisms because they cannot live without moisture.

Buying dried food

- Packaging should be intact
- Check the expiry date
- Check the list of ingredients

Labelling

The purpose of **food labelling** is to **inform** consumers about pre-packaged foods. The basic rule of labelling is that the consumer **must not be misled**.

Information on labels of packaged foods

European Union regulations state that the following information must appear on the label of pre-packaged foods:

- **Name of the product**
- **List of ingredients** in descending order of weight
- **Net quantity**
- **Date mark**: The product should be used by this date
- **Storage instructions**
- **Name and address of manufacturer**
- **Place of origin**

- **Instructions for use**: Preparation or cooking instructions
- **Nutrition information** is compulsory only if a nutritional claim is made on a product, e.g. low in fat

Advantages of nutrition information

- It is helpful for keeping a balanced diet
- People on special diets, such as low salt or high fibre, can make more informed choices
- People who suffer ill effects from certain types of food can avoid these foods

Date marking

There are two types of date marking:

- **Best before date:** This is the date up until the product can be expected to be in best condition. It is found on products with a long shelf life such as pasta and biscuits
- **Use-by date:** This is used on highly perishable foods with a short shelf life which need to be refrigerated. Examples include raw and cooked meats, milk and yoghurts

Unit pricing

This is the price per kilogram or litre. It is required on:

- Foods sold loose such as fruit and vegetables
- Pre-packaged foods sold in varying quantities such as cheese

Additives

Food additives are substances added to food by manufacturers in order to **improve** the food in some way.

Reasons for the use of food additives

Additives are used because they:
- Preserve food which makes it last longer
- Reduce the risk of food poisoning (preservatives)

- Improve the appearance and flavour of food
- Improve the texture of food
- Improve the food value of foods (nutritional additives)

> **Points to note**
>
> An **E number** means that the additive has been thoroughly tested by experts and has been accepted as safe in the EU.

Additives used in foods

Additive	Function	Examples
Colours (E100–E199)	They make food look more appealing	Carotene: Used in soft drinks Tartrazine (E102): Used in soft drinks
Flavourings (these do not have E numbers)	They improve the flavour of food	Sugar, salt and spices Saccharine and Aspartame are artificial sweeteners used in soft drinks
Flavour enhancers (E620–E640)	They make the existing flavour seem stronger	Monosodium glutamate (E621) Used in stock cubes
Preservatives (E200–E299)	They prevent the growth of microorganisms	Salt, vinegar and sorbic acid: Used in soft drinks
Antioxidants (E300–E399)	They prevent foods containing fat from going rancid (bad)	Vitamin C Vitamin E
Emulsifiers and stabilisers	Emulsifiers force oil and water to mix. Stabilisers prevent water and oil from separating	Emulsifier: Lecithin (E422) Stabiliser: Guar gum (E412)
Nutritive additives	They improve food value and replace nutrients lost during processing	Vitamins and minerals added to breakfast cereals

Advantages and disadvantages of additives

Advantages	Disadvantages
• They make food last longer and reduce waste • They allow a wider choice of foods • They preserve food and so reduce the risk of food poisoning • Good quality food can be provided consistently	• Additives may deceive the consumer • Some people suffer side effects such as migraine, skin rashes and hyperactivity • There is a danger that a mixture of additives may be harmful to the body over time • Some additives destroy vitamins in food

Convenience foods

Convenience foods are foods which are **partly or totally prepared** so that little effort is required to cook them.

Reasons for popularity of convenience foods

- Less time is required for preparation and cooking
- Advertising encourages the use of convenience foods
- Individual portions can be economical
- They produce very little waste
- There is a wide variety available

Ready-to-cook and cook-chill foods

- **Ready-to-cook foods** are very popular convenience foods. The food is prepared and then chilled. Some ready-to-cook foods are suitable for home freezing
- **Cook-chill foods** are cooked by the manufacturer and then chilled between 0°C and 4°C. They include foods such as Sauce Bolognaise and curries
- Ready-to-cook and cook-chill foods must be stored continuously at a temperature below 4°C in the shop and at home to prevent the growth of food-poisoning bacteria such as **listeria**

- Cook-chill foods must always be **reheated thoroughly** to destroy bacteria
- Foods reheated in a microwave should be stirred to ensure even reheating

Buying convenience foods

When buying convenience foods, check the:
- Expiry date
- Number of portions in the packet
- Cooking method required
- List of ingredients

Storing convenience foods

- Follow the instructions on the label. Perishable foods should be stored in a refrigerator
- Freeze only if the label states that the product is suitable for freezing
- Use before the expiry date

Guidelines for using convenience foods

- Follow cooking instructions exactly as they appear on the label
- Balance the use of convenience foods with fresh foods to avoid overusing convenience foods

- Choose good-quality convenience foods
- Read labels to check the sugar, fat and salt content of convenience foods

- Use convenience foods as a basis for more interesting dishes such as a scone mix for making pizza
- Follow the manufacturer's instructions exactly

Advantages and disadvantages of convenience foods

Advantages	Disadvantages
• They save time and energy • Very little skill required and therefore useful for those with poor cooking skills • They add interest to meals by including exotic ingredients • They can be fortified with vitamins and minerals • They can be useful in emergencies • They avoid waste	• They are often inferior in food value, colour and flavour when compared to fresh produce • They are expensive because of processing and packaging • They may contain lots of additives • They may contain excess sugar, salt and fat • Portion sizes are small • Overpackaging is wasteful and damaging to the environment

Sample exam question

Question

The following information is displayed on a frozen pizza box.

ITALIAN STYLE PIZZA

INGREDIENTS	NUTRITIONAL INFORMATION
Wheatflour, Cheddar and Mozzarella Cheese (20%), Water, Chicken (11%), Red Peppers (8%), Tomato, Onion, Vegetable Oil, Antioxidants, Sugar, Yeast, Salt, Herbs, Spices, Emulsifiers.	Average values per 100g Energy 233kcal/980kj Carbohydrates 27.2g Protein 11.4g Fat 8.7g Fibre 2.1g Sodium 0.5g
ITALIAN STYLE PIZZA	328g ℮

Question

(a) Evaluate the nutritive value of this frozen pizza.

(b) Set out a menu, to include pizza, suitable for a main meal for a teenager.

(c) Give two reasons why this pizza is not suitable for a vegan.

(d) (i) Name two food additives used in this pizza.

    (ii) Give the function of one of the food additives you have named.

(e) What symbol on this frozen pizza box indicates the place of origin?

(2002, HL)

Your revision notes

1.9 Digestion

●●●Learning Objectives

In this chapter you will learn to:
1 Identify the parts of the digestive system and state their functions
2 Explain the key terms associated with digestion and absorption of food
3 Describe the breakdown and absorption of food in the digestive system

Digestion means **breaking down food into tiny molecules** so that it can be used by the body. Food is broken down by **physical** and **chemical changes**.

Physical Change	Chemical Change
● The teeth **cut** and **grind** the food into smaller particles in the mouth ● The stomach **churns** the food into a smooth mixture called **chyme**	● This involves special chemicals called enzymes ● **Enzymes** break down proteins, fats and carbohydrates into smaller molecules ● Each enzyme works on **one** nutrient only. For example, the enzyme that works on protein does not work on fats

Enzymes change:
1 **Proteins** into **amino acids**
2 **Fats** into **fatty acids** and **glycerol**
3 **Carbohydrates** into simple sugars, e.g. **glucose**

Points to note

An **enzyme** is a chemical which causes a chemical change without changing itself.

Parts of Digestive System	What Happens?	Function
Mouth	The **teeth** cut and grind the food into smaller particles	Physical breakdown
	The food is mixed with saliva which contains an enzyme called **salivary amylase. Salivary amylase** changes starch into maltose	Chemical breakdown
Oesophagus	The food is pushed along this tube into the stomach by a muscular movement called **peristalsis**	
Stomach	The stomach stores the food and **churns** it into a smooth liquid called **chyme**	Physical breakdown
	A liquid called **gastric juice** is released from the lining of the stomach. Gastric juice contains an acid called hydrochloric acid and an enzyme called **pepsin**.	Chemical breakdown
	Pepsin changes **protein** to **peptide chains**	
Liver	The gall bladder in the liver produces **bile**, which helps to break down fats	
Pancreas	Produces enzymes	
Small intestine	**Proteins** and peptides are changed into **amino acids**	Chemical breakdown
	Sugars are changed into **simple sugars**	
	Fats are changed into **fatty acids** and **glycerol**	
	The digested food is **absorbed** into the bloodstream through tiny hair-like fingers called **villi**	Absorption
	Glucose and amino acids go directly into the blood	
	Fatty acids and glycerol go into the **lymph system** first and then into the blood stream	

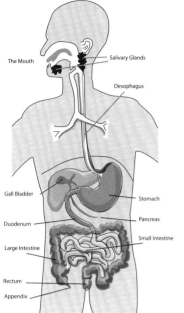

The Mouth

Salivary Glands

Oesophagus

Gall Bladder

Stomach

Duodenum

Pancreas

Small Intestine

Large Intestine

Rectum

Appendix

Parts of Digestive System	What Happens?	Function
Large intestine	Faeces are pushed along the large intestine by **peristalsis**	
	Water is reabsorbed into the bloodstream	Reabsorption of water
	Produces **Vitamin K** and **B group vitamins**	Manufacture of vitamins
	Waste is removed when muscles in the rectum force the faeces out of the body through the anus	Elimination of waste

Points to note

Absorption is the passing of digested food from the small intestine into the bloodstream. The **blood transports** the digested food around the body where it is used in the cells for growth and energy.

Sample exam question

Question

(a) State the function of each of the following parts of the digestive system:
  (i)   the mouth;
  (ii) the stomach;
  (iii) the small intestine.
(b) Describe two physical changes and two chemical changes which occur during digestion.
(c) Explain what is meant by *peristalsis*.
(d) What is the role of fibre in digestion?

(2003, HL)

2.1 Consumers' rights and responsibilities

●●●Learning Objectives

In this chapter you will learn to:
1 Define a consumer
2 Differentiate between goods and services
3 Differentiate between needs and wants
4 List and explain consumers' rights and responsibilities

- A **consumer** is anyone who buys goods or uses services
- **Goods** are things such as food, clothes and cars
- A **service** is work done for payment, e.g. hairdressing, public transport, supply of electricity
- **Needs** are what we must have to survive, e.g. food, clothing and shelter
- **Wants** are the extras that may make life more pleasant or comfortable
- A **right** is something you are entitled to
- A **responsibility** is something you must do and for which you are answerable

Consumers' rights

1 The right to choice
2 The right to quality and value for money
3 The right to accurate information
4 The right to safety
5 The right to redress

Points to note

Redress may be one of the three **Rs**: a free repair, full or partial refund or a replacement.

Consumers' responsibilities

The consumer has the responsibility to:
1 Be informed
2 Examine goods and services
3 Read labels
4 Complain
5 Be environmentally aware

●●●Learning Objectives

In this chapter you will learn to:

1 Identify and explain the following consumer laws: The Sale of Goods and Supply of Services Act 1980; the Consumer Information Act 1978
2 Name the following statutory agencies for consumer protection: The Director of Consumer Affairs and Fair Trade; the Ombudsman; the Small Claims Registrar/Court
3 Name the following voluntary agencies for consumer protection: Trade associations; Consumers' Association of Ireland
4 Identify sources of consumer information
5 Explain how to complain and demonstrate how to write a letter of complaint

Consumer protection is necessary to:
● Protect consumers' rights
● Give a means of redress
● Guard against exploitation

Points to note

REVISE WISE
POINTS TO NOTE

When you buy goods and services, a **contract** is set up between the buyer and the seller. Under this contract the seller has duties to the consumer. The contract is **not** between the consumer and the manufacturer of the goods.

The Sale of Goods and Supply of Services Act 1980

All **goods** should:
● Be of merchantable quality
● Be fit for their purpose
● Be as described
● Correspond with samples

Services should be provided by a skilled person, with proper care and diligence, and using sound materials.

A **guarantee** is a promise by the manufacturer that he/she will make good any faults in an item for a specific period of time after purchase.

The Consumer Information Act 1978

The Act protects consumers against false or misleading claims about goods, services or prices. It is an offence to:

- Make misleading claims about the price of goods
- Advertise a misleading price reduction
- Publish a misleading advertisement
- Make false or misleading claims about goods and services

Statutory agencies for consumer protection

- The **Director of Consumer Affairs and Fair Trade** enforces the law in relation to the sale of goods and services
- The **Ombudsman** deals with consumer complaints against government departments, health boards and An Post
- The **Small Claims Registrar/Court** deals quickly and cheaply with claims about goods and services where the value of the claim is less than €1,270

Voluntary agencies for consumer protection

- **Trade associations** operate a code of practice for dealing with consumer complaints about their members
- The **Consumers' Association of Ireland** is an independent non-profit association of consumers. It publishes the magazine *Consumer Choice*

Points to note

Consumer information is knowledge that helps consumers to make good decisions about how they will spend their money.

Consumer education helps consumers to use and apply consumer information in order to make the best decisions.

Sources of consumer information

1. The Director of Consumer Affairs
2. Consumers' Association of Ireland
3. The Ombudsman
4. Consumer programmes on TV and radio
5. Advertising
6. Manufacturers' leaflets and brochures

Remember ...

... 6 points.

Points to note

Some sources of information, e.g. word of mouth, are more available than others, while others, such as the Ombudsman, are very reliable and worthwhile.

How to complain

C   **C**omplain as soon as possible.
O   **O**nly complain to the seller or manager.
M   **M**ake your case clear.
P   **P**ersist and do not be fobbed off.
L   **L**et the seller know that you are aware of your rights.
A   **A**void losing your temper.
I   **I**ndicate how you wish to be compensated.
N   **N**ever play down your complaint.

Complain **in person, by telephone** or **by writing** a letter of complaint.

Sample letter of complaint

5 Sycamore Drive
Bray
Co. Dublin

20 August 2007   ← Date

The Customer Services Manager
Hadley's Sports
Main Street
Bray
Co. Dublin

Dear Sir,

I wish to complain about a pair of Nike Marauder T 90 football boots, which I bought in your shop on 29 July last (see copy of receipt enclosed).

After wearing the boots for two training sessions, the stitching on the side of the left boot started to come apart. This was a cause of great annoyance and inconvenience to me. I returned to your shop with the boots on 10 August and explained the situation to the shop assistant, who offered to return the boots to the manufacturer to be repaired.

This is unacceptable, as clearly there is a fault in the boots and by law, I am entitled to a full refund of the cost of the boots, which was €120.

Yours faithfully,
Owen Donovan

Customer's address

Name and address of Customer Services Manager

When and where product was bought and proof of purchase

Clear details of the complaint

Action you would like taken

Sample exam question

Question

Sarah bought a new steam iron and discovered that the iron was leaking when she used it.

(a) Outline the steps Sarah should follow when returning the faulty iron to the shop.

(b) Name two organisations that Sarah could contact if the shop refused to accept responsibility for the faulty iron.

(c) Write Sarah's letter of complaint to one of the organisations you have named.

(d) What conditions are outlined in the *Sale of Goods and Supply of Services Act 1980*?

(2004, HL)

Your revision notes

●●●Learning Objectives

In this chapter you will learn to:
1 Explain the meaning and purpose of a budget
2 Apply the management system to planning a budget
3 Explain the following terms: Gross income, net income, PAYE and PRSI
4 List the advantages of budgeting
5 Outline the steps in planning a budget
6 Explain the term 'credit buying'
7 List the advantages and disadvantages of buying on credit
8 State the benefits of a household filing system

A **budget** is a plan for spending money.

The **purpose of a budget** is to balance income with expenditure.

The **management system** may be applied to planning a budget as follows:
1 **Goal:** To balance income and expenditure
2 **Resources:** Resources such as money, time and energy will be needed to reach this goal
3 **Plan:** A budget or spending plan must be made out
4 **Action:** This plan must be put into action
5 **Evaluation:** The budget must be evaluated to check if the goal was reached, i.e. did the income balance with the expenditure?

Steps in planning a budget

1 Work out your weekly or monthly income in one column
2 Make a list of your weekly or monthly expenses and savings in a second column
3 Add the totals in each column and balance your budget
4 If your expenditure is greater than your income, you are overspending and need to make changes
5 If your income is greater than your expenditure, extra savings may be made

Points to note

Gross income is income earned before deductions.
Net income is income after deductions.
PAYE (Pay As You Earn) is a form of income tax.
PRSI (Pay Related Social Insurance) pays for benefits if you are unemployed or unable to work.

Advantages of budgeting

1 Security is provided and there will be fewer financial worries

Remember ...

... 5 points.

2 Maximum use is made of income
3 Overspending is highlighted
4 Good example is set for children
5 Allowance is made for large bills and seasonal spending

Saving

Credit unions, the post office, banks and building societies all provide options for saving money.

Buying on credit

- **Credit buying** means '**buy now, pay later**'

Sample exam questions

- Forms of credit include credit cards, bank loans, bank overdrafts and hire purchase

Advantages	Disadvantages
• The consumer has the use of the item before it is fully paid for • Some large items, e.g. houses or cars, could not be bought without credit	• Costs more as interest is charged • May lead to serious debt

Home filing

A home filing system is a useful and efficient way of storing important documents as it helps family members to find things easily, to compare past and current bills, to check fuel consumption or school progress, etc. Documents could be organised under different headings such as Mortgage, Insurance, Guarantees, School Reports and so on.

Question

1 Peter and Joan Murphy's daughter is going to attend post-primary school next year.
   (a) List three major expenses that the Murphys may have as a result.
   (b) Suggest two ways the Murphys might reduce these expenses.
   (c) Name two methods of saving which could be used to save for extra expenses.
   (d) State two advantages and two disadvantages of borrowing money.

   (2004, OL)

2 Ciara is about to start her first year at third level college. She plans to live in rented accommodation with three other students and share living expenses.
   (a) State the importance of budgeting for this group of students.
   (b) Set out five guidelines which the students should follow when planning their weekly budget.
   (c) Outline two benefits of keeping a filing system.

   (1998, HL)

●●●Learning Objectives

In this chapter you will learn to:
1 Explain the following terms: Quality, quality assurance, quality control and guarantee
2 Identify quality and standard marks
3 Illustrate how the quality of a service may be evaluated

- **Quality** is a term used to indicate that products or services are of a high standard
- **Quality assurance** is the system that ensures that the product will be of the quality required for its intended use
- **Quality control** is a series of strict tests a product undergoes to ensure that it reaches a certain standard

Quality and standard marks

The following quality and standard marks are awarded to goods and services that reach a high standard of quality.

Quality Mark	What Does It Mean?	Symbol
Guaranteed Irish	Product has been manufactured in Ireland to a high standard	guaranteed irish
Approved Quality System	Awarded by the Irish Quality Control Association	EIQA QUALITY CERTIFIED
Kitemark	Symbol of the British Standards Institution (BSI)	APPROVED TO BRITISH STANDARD

Quality Mark	What Does It Mean?	Symbol
Irish Standards Mark	Irish equivalent of the Kitemark. Awarded by the National Standards Authority of Ireland	
NSAI Mark	International quality standard awarded to companies with excellent quality management systems	
Pure New Wool (Woolmark)	Indicates that an item is made from 100% pure new wool	
Double Insulated Appliances	Earth wire is not required	
Communauté Européenne	Safety mark awarded by the EU	
BSI Safety Mark	British Standards Institution mark for safety	
Smoking Kills	A government health warning found on cigarette packets and advertisements	

Guarantees

A **guarantee** is a promise by the manufacturer that he/she will make good any faults in an item for a specific period of time after purchase.

Services

Remember ...

... 5 points for each.

To evaluate a service in terms of quality, consider the following:

🙂	🙁
1 Clean premises	1 Dirty premises
2 Clean toilet facilities	2 Poor toilet facilities
3 Well-managed	3 Disorganised staff
4 Friendly staff	4 Dismissive, unhelpful staff
5 Good personal hygiene	5 Careless personal hygiene

Your revision notes

2.5 Advertising

●●●**Learning Objectives**

In this chapter you will learn to:
1 Define advertising, marketing and market research
2 List the methods (sources) and functions of advertising
3 Analyse what makes an advertisement effective
4 State the advantages and disadvantages of advertising
5 Name the laws and the organisations which control advertising standards

Advertising is any message designed to inform, persuade or influence consumers.

Methods (sources) of advertising

1 TV and radio
2 Newspapers and magazines
3 Cinema, video and DVD
4 Buses, trams and bus shelters
5 Packets

Remember ...
... 5 points.

Functions of advertising

● To introduce new products
● To provide information on a product
● To promote brand names
● To increase sales

An effective advertisement should:
P Persuade the consumer to buy the product
I Interest the consumer
C Create desire
C Capture attention

Advantages and disadvantages of advertising

Remember ...
... 4 points for each.

Advantages	Disadvantages
1 Provides information	1 Increases prices of some goods
2 Provides employment	2 Billboards may spoil the landscape
3 Increases sales	3 Makes exaggerated claims
4 Keeps down the cost of newspapers and magazines	4 Encourages materialism

Control of advertising

Advertising is controlled in two ways: legal control and voluntary control.

Legal control

- **EU Misleading Advertising Regulations:** They protect the public against the effects of misleading advertising
- **Consumer Information Act 1978:** Makes it an offence to make false or misleading claims about goods and services
- **Employment Equality Act 1998:** Makes it illegal for advertisements to discriminate on the grounds of gender or marital status

Voluntary control

- **The Advertising Standards Authority for Ireland:** Encourages advertisers to follow a code of standards that states that all advertisements must be legal, decent, honest and truthful

- **The Central Copy Clearance (CCCI):** Reviews all alcohol advertisements in the Irish media

Marketing

- **Marketing** is the business of selling goods
- The **tools of marketing** are advertising, sales promotions, public relations, attractive packaging and presentation
- **Market research** involves the use of surveys to find out the public's likes and dislikes

Sample exam questions

Question

1 Advertising is a means of influencing the consumer to buy/use a particular product or service.
  (a) Name three methods of advertising.
  (b) Give two advantages and two disadvantages of advertising.

(1998, OL)

2 (a) List four sources of advertising.
  (b) Give three advantages and three disadvantages of advertising.
  (c) (i) Describe three marketing techniques used in supermarkets.
      (ii) Name the marketing technique you think is most effective and give a reason for your answer.
  (d) Outline the role of the Advertising Standards Authority for Ireland.

(2005, HL)

2.6 Shopping

edco home economics REVISE WISE

●●●**Learning Objectives**

In this chapter you will learn to:
1 Summarise the decision-making process
2 List the factors to consider when choosing a product
3 Name and give examples of different types of shopping outlets
4 Compare counter service and self-service
5 Summarise the marketing techniques used in supermarkets to encourage buying
6 Compile a list of guidelines for wise shopping
7 List the functions and types of packaging
8 Discuss the characteristics of good packaging and comment on overpackaging
9 State the functions of product labelling
10 Explain the following terms: Bar code, unit pricing, loss leaders, bulk buying, own brands
11 Evaluate the following methods of payment: Cash, cheque, credit card, debit/laser card

The decision-making process

Before we go shopping, we make decisions about what we are going to buy and where we are going to buy it. The **decision-making process** involves the following steps:

D **Define** the decision to be made.
E **Enquire** about possible alternatives.
C **Consider** the alternatives.
I **Investigate** the consequences.
D **Decide** on a plan and put it into action.
E **Evaluate** the results.

The following **factors** influence our decisions:
1 Resources
2 Needs and wants
3 Values
4 Advertising
5 Other people
6 Fashion
7 Culture
8 Emotions
9 Merchandising

Remember ...

... 9 points.

When **choosing a product**, consider the following:

- **Budget:** Can you afford it?
- **Value:** Is it good value for money?
- **Purpose:** Is it necessary?
- **Environment:** Is it environmentally friendly?
- **Guarantee:** Does it have a guarantee?
- **Quality:** Is it well made?
- **Design:** Is it well designed?
- **Safety:** Is it safe to use?
- **Maintenance:** Is it easy to clean and look after?

Shopping outlets

There are many different types of shopping outlets:

1 Department stores, e.g. Marks & Spencer
2 Supermarkets, e.g. Tesco
3 Multiple chain stores, e.g. Dunnes Stores
4 Voluntary chains, e.g. Centra
5 Independent shops: Small and privately owned
6 Hypermarkets and superstores: Huge buildings which sell a vast range of goods
7 Boutiques: Specialist clothes shops
8 Discount stores, e.g. EuroCity
9 Specialist shops: Specialise in sports wear, shoes, jewellery, etc.

Counter service and self-service

	Counter Service	Self-service
Advantages	1 Personal service 2 Advice offered 3 Credit sometimes offered 4 Less effort for the shopper	1 Quick and convenient 2 Goods are well displayed 3 Wide range of products available 4 Prices are lower due to bulk buying
Disadvantages	1 Higher prices 2 More staff needed which leads to higher costs 3 Smaller selection of goods	1 Less personal contact 2 Credit usually not available 3 Possibility of long queues at checkouts

Marketing techniques

Here are some marketing techniques used by supermarkets to encourage the consumer to buy more:

1 Heavy goods at the entrance to encourage customers to use trolleys
2 Essentials at the farthest point from the entrance
3 Wide aisles
4 Luxuries at eye level
5 Sweets at the checkout

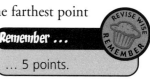

Remember ...

... 5 points.

Shopping guidelines

1　Make a list
2　Shop around
3　Avoid impulse buying
4　Look for quality and freshness
5　Keep receipts

Remember ...

... 5 points.

Packaging

Due to changes in consumer buying habits and the increasing number of convenience foods on the market, the amount of packaging used has also increased.

Functions of packaging

1　Protects goods
2　Provides information
3　Keeps products (food) fresh
4　Advertises the product
5　Carries bar codes

Types of packaging

- Glass
- Paper
- Metal
- Plastic

Characteristics of good packaging

1　Strong
2　Light
3　Hygienic
4　Easy to open
5　Waterproof
6　Non-toxic
7　Biodegradable

Disadvantages of packaging/overpackaging

- Uses up natural resources
- Adds to the price
- May be difficult to open
- Can be deceptive
- Causes litter
- Aerosols may be dangerous

Points to note

As a consumer, **reduce, reuse and recycle** in order to cut down on the damaging effects of packaging on the environment.

Product labelling

Product labelling is important to:
1　**Identify** products
2　**Advertise** products
3　**Describe** ingredients/components
4　**Warn** of any dangers
5　**Give advice** on use
6　**Tell** where product was made
7　**Carry bar codes**

Points to note

A **bar code** is a series of bars and spaces which can be read by electronic scanners. It gives details of products bought and ensures that till receipts are more accurate.

Marketing terms

Unit pricing	Goods are priced according to a unit of measurement, e.g. per kg or per litre
Loss leaders	Products sold at a loss in order to attract customers to a shop
Bulk buying	Buying large quantities of a product because it is cheaper
Own brands	Goods which carry the shop's own brand name, e.g. St Bernard, Tesco. Simply packaged and often cheaper than similar branded products

Methods of payment

Cash	Quick and easy Inconvenient for expensive goods May be lost or stolen
Cheque and cheque card	Safer and more convenient than cash Current account required to write cheques Easy to overspend
Credit card	Safe and convenient Interest free if balance is cleared on time If not, high rate of interest is charged Easy to overspend
Debit/laser card	Payment is taken from customer's current account Cash back available Safe and convenient Current account required

Sample exam questions

Question

1 (a) List three guidelines that consumers should follow when shopping.
   (b) List three items of information that you would expect to find on a receipt.
   (c) Explain the term 'bulk buying'.

(2004, OL)

2 (a) Compare and evaluate
        (i) shopping in a large multiple chain store with (ii) shopping in
        a small specialist shop with regard to each of the following:
        (i)   personal service
        (ii)   convenience
        (iii) value for money
        (iv)   methods of payment
        (v)   availability of credit
   (b) Describe four techniques used by shops to encourage the consumer to spend
        more money.
   (c) Comment on the overpackaging of consumer products.

(1996, HL)

Your revision notes

3.1 Family, roles, relationships, new life, growth and development

●●●Learning Objectives

In this chapter you will learn to:
1. Explain the terms 'nuclear family' and 'extended family'
2. List the functions of the family
3. Explain the terms 'gender role', 'stereotype' and 'gender equality'
4. Describe the male and female reproductive systems
5. Explain the terms associated with reproduction
6. List guidelines which promote good health during pregnancy
7. Describe the various types of human development
8. Explain the terms 'peer group', 'peer pressure', 'assertiveness' and 'norm'

The family

- A **family** is a group of people who are related by blood, marriage or adoption
- The **nuclear family** consists of parents and their children
- The **extended family** consists of parents and children together with other relatives

Functions of the family

The family provides for our:
- **Physical needs:** Food, clothing, shelter
- **Emotional needs:** Love and security
- **Economic needs:** Family members share money and other possessions

Influences on family life

- **Cultural factors** such as religion and language
- **Social factors** such as educational opportunities
- **Economic factors** such as money available

Rights of children

Children have the right to:
- Love and security
- Care
- Education
- Protection from neglect or abuse

Roles

- A **role** is the way we are expected to behave
- **Gender role** or **sex role** means the way one is expected to behave because of one's gender
- Gender roles are **learned** at **home**, at **school** and in the **community**
- A **stereotype** is a fixed image of how people should behave
- **Gender equality** means equal treatment of males and females

Role of parents

Parents must ensure that the physical and emotional needs of their children are provided for.

Relationships

The relationship between a parent and a child is extremely important. Children need to have a good relationship with their parents in order to feel secure and confident.

Communication

- Relationships are based on **communication**.
- Communication can be **verbal** (using words) or **non-verbal** (without words)
- **Listening** is the most important skill in communication.

Conflict

Conflict arises because people see the same situation differently.

Points to note

The **Irish Society for Prevention of Cruelty to Children (ISPCC)** is an organisation which offers support to teenagers. They provide a helpline called *Childline*.

New life

Female sex organs

The functions of the female sex organs are to:

- Produce the eggs
- Provide a safe place for the baby to develop

Organ	Function
Ovaries	Produce and store the eggs
Fallopian tubes	Link the ovaries to the womb (uterus)
Uterus (womb)	Where the developing baby grows until birth
Vagina	Birth canal

Ovulation

- **Ovulation** is the monthly release of an egg from one of the ovaries
- The egg travels along the fallopian tube towards the uterus (womb)
- If the egg is fertilised it will bury itself in the thickened lining of the uterus

Menstruation

If the egg is not fertilised, the unwanted lining of the uterus flows out of the body. This is called **menstruation.**

> **Points to note**
>
> The **female sex hormones** are called **oestrogen** and **progesterone**. They control sexual development, ovulation and menstruation.

Male sex organs

The functions of the male sex organs are to:
- Produce sperm
- Place the sperm inside the woman's body

Organ	Function
Testicles	Make and store sperm
Scrotum	Pouch of skin which contains the testicles
Sperm ducts	Carry sperm to the penis
Penis	Transfers sperm into the woman's body

> **Points to note**
>
> The **male sex hormone** is called **testerone**. It controls sexual development and production of sperm.

Sexual intercourse

- During sexual intercourse the penis becomes stiff
- The penis is inserted into the woman's vagina
- Semen, which contains the sperm, is released into the vagina

Fertilisation

Sperm swim up through the vagina into the womb and into the fallopian tubes. **Fertilisation** occurs **when a sperm joins with an egg.**

Pregnancy

- The fertilised egg travels to the womb where it implants itself
- It is now called an **embryo**
- The embryo is protected in the womb by **amniotic fluid**
- After about 8 weeks the developing baby is called a **foetus**

The placenta

- The umbilical cord joins the foetus to the mother at the **placenta**
- **Oxygen and nutrients** pass **from the mother** to the foetus at the placenta
- **Waste substances**, such as carbon dioxide and urea, also pass **from the foetus** to the mother through the placenta

> **Points to note**
>
> For a **healthy pregnancy**:
> - Refrain from smoking
> - Avoid alcohol
> - Avoid all drugs except medicines prescribed by a doctor
> - Eat a healthy diet

Birth

- The bag of amniotic fluid bursts
- The muscles of the womb begin to contract and the cervix opens
- The baby moves along the vagina, usually head first
- Once the baby comes out, the umbilical cord is clamped and cut
- The placenta passes out of the mother's body. This is called **afterbirth**

Responsible sexual behaviour

Casual sex can cause:
- Unwanted pregnancy
- Low self-esteem
- Sexually transmitted infections (STIs)

Growth and development

Types of development

1 **Physical development**
   - Children grow continuously as they get older
   - At **puberty** the growth is more obvious as children begin to change into adults
   - Puberty is the beginning of **adolescence**. During adolescence boys and girls become sexually mature
   - Hormones account for the changes at puberty
   - Changes in girls at puberty include breast development and menstruation
   - Changes in boys at puberty include 'wet dreams' and growth of facial hair

2 **Mental or intellectual development**
   - Mental or intellectual development is the development of the mind

3 **Emotional development**
   - Emotional development involves learning to manage your feelings or emotions

- The most important part of emotional development is **self-esteem**

Points to note

Having high **self-esteem** means that you believe in your own self-worth. You feel confident, accepted and assertive.

Assertiveness means being able to express with confidence what you want.

- **Factors** which contribute to emotional development include:
  (i) Being accepted by others
  (ii) Being treated fairly
  (iii) Communication with others
- **Emotional maturity** means being able to:
  (i) Handle feelings of **love, anger** and **fear**
  (ii) Develop relationships
  (iii) Develop talents

4 **Personality development**
   - Personality is part of our identity. Personality is determined by:
     (i) **Heredity:** Personality traits are inherited from parents
     (ii) **Environment:** People around you influence your personality

5 **Social development**
   - Social development involves learning **how to deal with people in various situations**

6 **Moral development**
   - Moral development means being aware of **what is right and what is wrong**

Points to note

A **norm** is an acceptable way of behaving in our society.

Peer group

A peer group is a **group of people of the same age with similar interests**.

Peer pressure

Peer pressure means being expected to copy others in the peer group.

Sample exam question

Question

Adolescence is a time of change.
(a) Outline three physical changes that occur in boys and three physical changes that occur in girls during puberty.
(b) List four guidelines that an adolescent should follow in order to maintain good personal hygiene.
(c) Describe two positive and two negative ways in which adolescents can be influenced by their peers.
(d) Name one organisation which offers support to teenagers and briefly outline how this support is provided.

(2002, HL)

Your revision notes

3.2 The body

●●●**Learning Objectives**

In this chapter you will learn to:
1 Name the organs and describe the functions of
    (a) The respiratory (breathing) system
    (b) The circulatory (blood) system
2 Describe the structure and functions of skin and teeth
3 Outline guidelines for care of skin and teeth

The respiratory (breathing) system

- The removal of waste from the body is called **excretion**
- The **lungs remove carbon dioxide and water** from the body

The breathing system

We inhale (take in) oxygen from the air.

⬇

Oxygen combines with food to give us energy **(oxidation)**.

⬇

The waste products carbon dioxide and water are formed as a result of oxidation.

⬇

We exhale (breathe out) these waste products.

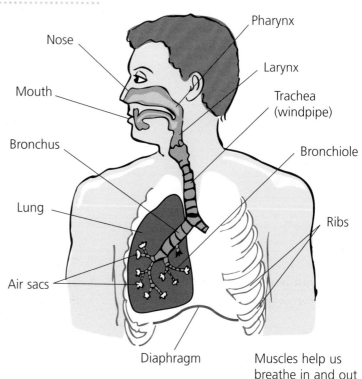

Nose

Mouth

Bronchus

Lung

Air sacs

Diaphragm

Pharynx

Larynx

Trachea (windpipe)

Bronchiole

Ribs

Muscles help us breathe in and out

Structure of the breathing system

Organ	Function
Nose ↓	Used to filter and warm the air
Pharynx: A space at the back of the mouth which contains a flap of skin called the epiglottis ↓	The epiglottis covers the opening of the trachea so that food does not get in
Larynx (voice box): Contains the vocal cords ↓	This produces sounds (voice) when air passes over the vocal cords
Trachea (windpipe): This flexible tube is lined with tiny hairs and is held open by rings of cartilage ↓	The hairs trap dust and germs which are sent back upwards, away from the lungs
Bronchus: The trachea divides into two tubes called the bronchi (singular: bronchus) ↓	Carries the air to the bronchioli
Bronchioli: The bronchi divide several times to form very narrow tubes called bronchioli (singular: bronchiole) ↓	Carries the air to the alveoli
Alveoli: At the end of the bronchioli are the air sacs or alveoli (singular: alveolus)	Oxygen reaches the blood and carbon dioxide is removed

The lungs

Position of the lungs

- The lungs are in the chest
- They are surrounded by the rib cage, the breast bone and the back bone
- The heart is between the lungs

Functions of the lungs

The lungs have the following functions:
- To take oxygen into the body
- To remove carbon dioxide from the body
- To remove water from the body

Exchange of gases

- The alveoli (air sacs) have very thin walls
- They are covered with capillaries (tiny blood vessels)
- Oxygen passes from the air sacs into the blood in the capillaries
- Carbon dioxide passes from the blood into the air sacs

Effects of smoking on the lungs

- Lung cancer
- Difficulty in breathing
- Production of excess mucus
- Diseases such as emphysema

The circulatory (blood) system

Blood

Blood consists of:
- A liquid called plasma
- Red blood cells
- White blood cells
- Blood platelets
- Dissolved substances such as digested foods, oxygen and carbon dioxide

Red blood cells

1 Red blood cells carry oxygen and carbon dioxide around the body
2 **Haemoglobin** (the red pigment in red blood cells) combines with oxygen and carries it all around the body in the blood
3 Iron is needed to make haemoglobin

White blood cells

White blood cells fight bacteria to protect the body from disease.

Blood platelets

Blood platelets help to clot the blood to stop bleeding.

Functions of the blood

- Blood **carries dissolved substances** around the body
- Blood **protects the body** from disease because white blood cells fight infection and platelets help clot the blood and stop bleeding
- Blood helps to **control body temperature** by carrying heat around the body and giving off heat when the body becomes too hot
- Blood **transports** hormones and enzymes around the body

Blood vessels

Arteries	Veins	Capillaries
<ul><li>Arteries carry blood **away from the heart**</li><li>The walls of the arteries are **thick** and **elastic**</li></ul>	<ul><li>Veins carry blood **towards the heart**</li><li>Veins have **thinner** walls than arteries</li><li>Veins have **valves** which prevent the blood from flowing backwards</li></ul>	<ul><li>Capillaries are tiny blood vessels which **link arteries and veins**</li><li>Capillary walls are only **one cell thick** so that oxygen and carbon dioxide can pass through them</li></ul>

The heart

The heart is positioned:
- In the middle of the chest
- Between the lungs
- Behind the ribs

The heart is made of **cardiac muscle**.

Parts of the heart

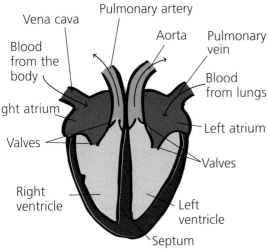

Vena cava

Pulmonary artery

Aorta

Pulmonary vein

Blood from the body

Blood from lungs

ght atrium

Valves

Left atrium

Valves

Right ventricle

Left ventricle

Septum

Sample exam question

Blood flow through the heart

1 Blood returns to the heart from around the body
2 This blood enters the **right atrium** through the vena cava
3 It then passes to the **right ventricle** before it is pumped to the lungs to pick up oxygen
4 Oxygen-rich blood from the lungs enters the **left atrium** by the pulmonary veins
5 This oxygen-rich blood then passes into the **left ventricle**
6 It is then pumped out through the aorta to the rest of the body
7 The coronary arteries supply blood to the heart itself

Points to note

Coronary heart disease occurs when the coronary arteries become clogged with fatty deposits.

Pulse

A **pulse** is a heartbeat which can be felt where an artery is close to the skin.

Question

(a) Name the parts of the heart labelled 1, 2, 3, 4 and 5.
(b) Describe the position of the heart in the body.
(c) List the functions of the blood.
(d) Name three blood vessels and outline the differences between any two of the blood vessels you have named.
(e) Explain how a person's *pulse* is taken.

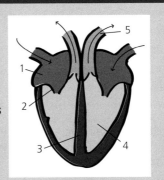

(2004, HL)

The skin

- The skin is an **excretory organ**
- It **removes waste** (sweat) from the body

The skin is made up of two layers:
- The **epidermis** (outer layer)
- The **dermis** (inner layer)

Parts of the skin

Part of Skin	Function
Dead cells	
Malpighian layer	Contains pigment that protects the skin from the sun
Sweat glands	Remove water and salt (sweat) through the pores
Blood vessels	Carry blood
Nerves	Enable us to feel cold, heat and pain
Oil glands and hair follicles	Oil keeps the skin soft Hairs keep the body warm
Fat cells	Keep the body warm

EPIDERMIS

DERMIS

Functions of the skin

- It **removes** excess water and salts in the form of **sweat**
- It **controls** body heat
- It **prevents** disease from entering the body
- It **protects** the body from harmful rays of the sun
- It allows us to **feel** heat, cold and pain
- **Vitamin D** is made in the skin

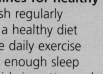

Points to note

Guidelines for healthy skin
- Wash regularly
- Eat a healthy diet
- Take daily exercise
- Get enough sleep
- Avoid cigarettes and alcohol
- Avoid overexposure to the sun

Body odour

- **Bacteria** on the skin work on **sweat** which causes **body odour**
- An unpleasant odour is produced if the skin is not washed
- **Deodorants** help prevent body odour
- **Antiperspirants** prevent perspiration (sweating)

Acne

Extra oil produced in the skin blocks pores, and bacteria on the skin cause infection.

Points to note

Guidelines to help prevent acne
- Do not squeeze or pick spots
- Clean skin thoroughly using antiseptic soap
- Avoid fatty foods
- If using medication against acne follow instructions carefully

Sample exam question

Question

(a) Name the parts of the skin labelled
   1, 2, 3 and 4.
(b) Give three functions of the skin.
(c) What causes body odour?
(d) List five guidelines that you would follow
   to ensure good personal hygiene.
   (2001, OL)

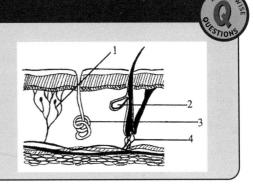

The teeth

- A young child has 20 primary
  (milk) teeth
- An adult has 32 permanent teeth

Functions of teeth

- Healthy teeth are attractive
- They enable us to speak properly
- They help to digest food

Unhealthy teeth can cause the following
problems:

- Bad breath
- Infections in the mouth and gums
- Stomach infections

Structure of a tooth

Crown

Root

Enamel
(protects the tooth)

Dentine
(softer than
enamel)

Pulp cavity
(contains blood
vessels and
nerves)

Cementum
(holds the tooth
in place)

Types of teeth

There are four types of teeth.

Type of Tooth	Shape and Function
Incisors	Sharp teeth used to bite and cut food
Canines (eye teeth)	Pointed teeth used to tear food
Pre-molars	Double-pointed teeth used to chew and grind food
Molars	Large flat teeth used to chew and grind food

Plaque and tooth decay

- Plaque consists of food particles, saliva and bacteria
- Plaque builds up on the surfaces of the teeth
- If plaque is not removed, **bacteria** present act on food to produce acids
- The acids attack tooth enamel, causing tooth decay
- The main cause of tooth decay is sugar consumption

Points to note

Guidelines for healthy teeth
- Avoid sugary snacks and drinks
- Brush teeth properly
- Visit your dentist regularly
- Replace your toothbrush every 3 months
- Use dental floss
- Eat a healthy diet

Sample exam question

Question

(a) The diagram shows an adult's permanent teeth.
   (i) Name the types of permanent teeth labelled A, B, C and D.
   (ii) State one function of each type.

(b) Explain the importance of healthy teeth.

(c) Describe the role of plaque in tooth decay.

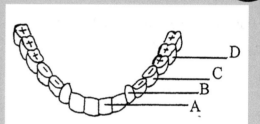

(d) What are the benefits of using each of the following dental hygiene products:
   (i)   Antiseptic mouthwash
   (ii) Flouride toothpaste
   (iii) Dental floss

(2001, HL)

3.3 Health and health hazards

●●●Learning Objectives

In this chapter you will learn to:
1 Outline the factors which contribute to health
2 Outline the benefits of exercise and leisure
3 Compile a list of guidelines to reduce the risk of coronary heart disease
4 Explain the term 'addiction'
5 Outline the reasons why some people smoke, drink and abuse drugs
6 Outline the harmful effects of smoking, drinking and drug abuse

Health

Health is physical and mental well-being. It is our responsibility to take care of our health.

Factors which contribute to health

- Precautions against disease
- Healthy diet
- Personal hygiene
- Physical exercise
- Rest and sleep
- Avoiding health hazards, e.g. drugs and alcohol
- A positive attitude

Mental health

Good mental health means **feeling positive** and having the **ability to cope** with everyday life.

Factors which contribute to good mental health are:
- Balancing work and relaxation
- Spending time with people whose company you enjoy
- Taking regular exercise
- Talking about your worries with someone you trust
- Making the most of your talents
- Seeking help for problems if necessary

Precautions against disease

Some diseases or conditions can be prevented by:
- Screening and developmental tests for babies
- Health checks for adults
- **Immunisation** or **vaccination** against disease

Physical exercise

Aerobic exercise

- Aerobic exercise is exercise which **makes you breathe faster**, e.g. running
- It **makes your heart and lungs work harder**
- Aerobic exercise helps prevent heart disease and high blood pressure

Benefits of regular exercise

Regular exercise:
- Helps to reduce and maintain a healthy weight
- Reduces the risk of heart disease and stroke
- Helps to control blood pressure
- Creates a 'feel good' factor
- Reduces stress
- Is a way of socialising
- Helps you to sleep better

Points to note

Guidelines to help maintain fitness and health
- Choose an activity which you **like**
- Exercise with friends if it is more fun
- Exercise for at least 30 minutes every day
- Stretch your muscles before exercising

Rest and sleep

It is essential for the body to rest because otherwise we would 'burn out'. Adequate sleep has the following benefits:
- We **work** better
- We **look** better
- We have better **concentration** levels
- It improves our **mood**

Insomnia is the inability to sleep.

Importance of leisure

Leisure time is **time to unwind** after school or work. It is the time when you **choose** to do activities which you **like**.
Leisure time:
- Reduces stress
- Allows you to learn new things
- Enables you to meet new people
- Reduces boredom
- Can allow you become fit

Coronary heart disease

Coronary heart disease occurs when **the arteries of the heart become blocked with a fatty substance called cholesterol.**

Factors which increase the risk of heart disease

- Heredity (runs in one's family)
- High-fat diet
- Overweight
- Lack of exercise
- Smoking
- Stress
- Too much alcohol

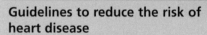

Points to note

Guidelines to reduce the risk of heart disease
- Avoid a high-fat diet
- Avoid being overweight
- Take plenty of exercise
- Avoid smoking
- Reduce stress
- Avoid too much alcohol

Points to note

The **Health Promotion Unit** is an organisation concerned with health promotion. It is run by the Department of Health and Children.

Health hazards

Smoking

An **addiction** is an **uncontrollable craving for a drug**. Nicotine is a **drug found in cigarettes** which causes addiction.

Reasons why some young people smoke:
- Peer pressure
- Curiosity
- Advertising
- Image

Harmful substances in cigarettes
- **Nicotine:** Causes **addiction**
- **Tar:** Clings to the lining of the lungs, making breathing difficult
- **Tobacco smoke:** Reduces the blood's ability to carry **oxygen** around the body
- **Irritants:** Cause **smoker's cough**

Harmful effects of smoking
- Lung cancer
- Breathing difficulties
- Heart disease
- High blood pressure
- Emphysema (a respiratory disease)
- Damage to unborn babies

Passive smoking

Passive smoking occurs when non-smokers inhale smoke from smokers' cigarettes.

Government controls
- It is illegal to sell cigarettes to people under 18
- Smoking is not permitted in any place of work
- Cigarette smoking is not allowed on TV
- Cigarette packets carry a government health warning
- There are high taxes on cigarettes and tobacco

Alcohol

Reasons why people drink:
- Many young people **experiment** with drink
- **Peer pressure** forces people to fit in with their friends
- People drink to overcome **shyness**
- People drink to **relax**
- People want to have a **'cool' image**

Short-term effects of drinking
- A person cannot think clearly and may take risks
- Co-ordination and judgement are lost
- People lose self-control
- Very heavy drinking can cause unconsciousness and even death

Long-term effects of alcohol abuse on the body
- A person can become addicted to alcohol
- Brain cells are permanently damaged
- Cancers may develop
- A person may become depressed
- Unborn babies are damaged if the mother is drinking during pregnancy

Points to note

Help available
- **Alcoholics Anonymous** is an organisation which helps people who suffer from alcoholism
- **Al Anon** helps the families of alcoholics
- **Al Ateen** helps the children of alcoholics

REVISE WISE POINTS TO NOTE

Drugs

A **drug** is a chemical that changes how the body functions physically, mentally or emotionally.

Common drugs include:
- Alcohol
- Caffeine
- Nicotine in cigarettes

Reasons why people take drugs:
- Curiosity
- Peer pressure
- Escape from boredom or worry
- Image
- Effect: People enjoy the effect that the drug has on them

Controlled drugs

Drugs which are available by prescription from a doctor are called controlled drugs.

Drug abuse

Drug abuse is the use of a drug which **damages some aspect of a person's life.**

Effects of drug abuse on the body:
- **Addiction** occurs, which means that the person suffers an uncontrollable desire for the drug
- **Dependence** occurs when the person depends on the drug to make him/her feel good
- **AIDS** is spread through sharing needles
- **Death** is often the result of an overdose

Effects of drug abuse on the family and society:
- Family disruption
- Crime
- Money is wasted
- Absenteeism from school and work

Sample exam question

Question

A healthy lifestyle contributes to the health and well-being of the young adult.
(a) Give three reasons why leisure is important in a teenager's lifestyle.
(b) State the possible effects on the body of each of the following:
    (i)   a high fat diet;
    (ii) smoking *and*
    (iii) stress.
(c) What do you understand by the term *coronary heart disease*?
(d) (i) What is aerobic exercise?
    (ii) Give two examples of aerobic exercise that you would recommend for teenagers.

(2000, HL)

edco home economics REVISE WISE

●●●Learning Objectives

In this chapter you will learn to:
1 Explain the following terms: Management, home management, goal, resource
2 Apply the management system to the management of the home
3 Evaluate the importance of work plans when managing the home

Management terms

- **Management** is the skilful use of time, energy and other resources
- **Home management** is the efficient running of the home
- A **goal** is what we want to achieve
- A **resource** is something we can use to help us achieve our goals

Home management

A management system can be used in the management of the home. It involves the following steps:
1 **Goals:** What needs to be done, e.g. shopping, cooking, cleaning
2 **Resources:** These are used to achieve goals. They include time, energy, people to help, equipment and money
3 **Plan:** The steps to be followed and the resources to be used to achieve the goals
4 **Action:** The plan is put into action
5 **Evaluation:** The outcome of the plan is examined and suggestions are made for any improvements

Work plans are important when managing the home. They ensure that:
- Jobs are done regularly
- All family members are involved
- The needs of the household are met

Here are some **guidelines** for drawing up work plans or routines:
1 Make a list of all the jobs that need to be done daily, weekly and occasionally
2 Include some weekly tasks each day and an occasional task each week
3 Estimate the time it takes to do different jobs so that the workload is spread evenly
4 Include all family members
5 Place the jobs in a logical order which will suit the family's lifestyle
6 Try out the work plan for a couple of weeks to see if it is efficient
7 Work in an organised manner to save time and effort. For example, when cleaning a room:
   (a) Tidy
   (b) Sweep (if not vacuuming)
   (c) Dust
   (d) Vacuum
   (e) Wash
   (f) Polish

4.2 Home and community

●●●**Learning Objectives**

In this chapter you will learn to:
1 List housing options
2 List and explain the human needs a home provides for
3 Explain and give examples of amenities and community services

People choose to live close to their place of work, schools, shops and other amenities.

Housing options include:
- Houses
- Apartments or flats
- Bedsits
- Residential accommodation (old people's homes, convents)
- Caravans, mobile homes, houseboats
- Sheltered housing (housing built for the elderly or disabled)

A **home** provides for many of our basic human **needs**:
1 **Physical needs:** Shelter, warmth and protection
2 **Emotional needs:** Safety, security, privacy and a caring and relaxing environment
3 **Social needs:** A place for entertaining and recreation

When people live together in an area, they form a **community**. All communities have services and amenities.
- An **amenity** is a useful or pleasant facility, e.g. community centres, beaches, shops
- **Community services** are provided by state (statutory) and voluntary organisations

Statutory Services	Voluntary Services
• Gardaí	• GAA
• Education (schools)	• St Vincent de Paul
• Health (hospitals)	• ISPCC
• Public housing	• Meals on Wheels
• Public libraries	• Youth clubs

4.3 Design and room planning

●●●**Learning Objectives**

In this chapter, you will learn to:
1 List and explain the following features of good design: Function, colour, form, texture and pattern
2 Explain the following design principles: Emphasis, balance, proportion and rhythm
3 List the factors to consider when planning rooms
4 Explain the following terms: Ergonomics, work sequence, work triangle

Features of design

Everything we wear, travel in, live in and use in our daily lives has been designed. When designing a home and its contents, the following features are all equally important:

- **Function:** An item must be designed to do a particular job
- **Colour:** This is one of the first design features we notice
- **Form:** This includes shape (the outline of an object, e.g. square or circle) and line (vertical, horizontal or diagonal)
- **Texture:** This describes the 'feel' of an object which may be rough or smooth
- **Pattern:** This is a decorative design used to provide interest and contrast, e.g. print, floral or check

Design principles

The following design principles or rules will help to create good results in home design:

- **Emphasis:** Part of the design stands out from it and draws the eye

- **Balance:** An equal spread of colour, pattern and texture in the room
- **Proportion:** The relationship between the sizes of different items in the room
- **Rhythm:** A regular or repeated colour or pattern in the design which links each part of the room

Room planning

When planning the layout of a room, consider the following:
1 Function of the room
2 Fixtures and fittings
3 Heating and lighting
4 Ventilation
5 Comfort
6 Aspect (the direction the room faces)
7 Storage space required
8 Traffic flow
9 Likes and dislikes of the occupants

Remember ...

... 9 points.

Planning a kitchen

The kitchen is one of the busiest rooms in the home and so demands very careful planning to ensure efficiency, comfort and safety. The layout of a kitchen is a very good example of **ergonomics** in action.

Points to note

Ergonomics is the study of the **efficiency of people in their workplace**. It involves designing equipment and room layouts to suit people so that time or energy will not be wasted.

When designing kitchens, the **work sequence** and **work triangle** must be considered.

- When preparing food, the **work sequence** involves the following steps:

STORAGE ➡ PREPARATION ➡ COOKING ➡ SERVING

Kitchen units and equipment should be arranged to follow the work sequence, regardless of whether the kitchen is laid out in a U-shape, L-shape or any other type of layout.

- The **work triangle** is an imaginary triangle which links the three main pieces of equipment in the kitchen, i.e. the refrigerator, cooker and sink

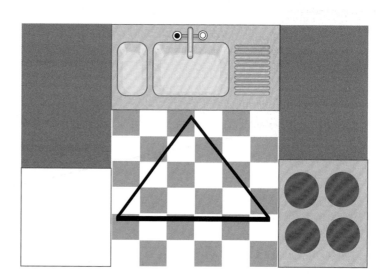

Example of a work triangle

Sample exam questions

Question

1 (a) Give four guidelines that should be considered when planning the layout of a room.
   (b) List five different family activities that take place in a living room.
   (c) Bearing in mind these activities, sketch and label the layout for a family living room.
   (d) State where you would include pattern in the living room you have planned.

   (1996, OL)

2 (a) List the factors that should be considered when decorating a family living room.
   (b) Draw the room plan and indicate on the plan the position of:
       (i)   the window(s);
       (ii) the door(s);
       (iii) the furniture and
       (iv) suitable lighting.
   (c) Suggest
       (i)   a colour scheme,
       (ii) a floor covering and
       (iii) a heating system suitable for the living room and give a reason for your suggestion in each case.
   (d) Explain the term *upholstery*.

   (2004, HL)

4.4 Safety and first aid

●●●**Learning Objectives**

In this chapter you will learn to:
1 List the causes of accidents in the home
2 Compile a list of guidelines for the prevention of accidents in the home
3 Describe how to carry out a fire drill in the home
4 Identify hazard symbols used on household chemicals
5 State the aims of first aid
6 List the contents of a first aid kit
7 Describe the first aid procedures for the following: Burns and scalds, shock, choking, cuts, falls and poisoning

Causes of accidents

- **People:** Carelessness, untidiness, curiosity, slow reactions
- **Buildings:** Bad design and maintenance, poor lighting
- **Objects:** Faulty equipment, incorrect storage of dangerous substances

Prevention of accidents

Remember ...
... 4 points for each.

Electricity

1 Never handle anything electrical with wet hands
2 Avoid trailing flexes
3 Never overload sockets or repair frayed flexes
4 Never take anything electrical into the bathroom

Fire

1 Use a fireguard around open fires
2 Install smoke alarms and test them regularly
3 Keep a fire extinguisher and fire blanket in the house
4 Switch off and unplug electrical appliances at night

Falls

1 Ensure that toys and other small items are not left lying around on the floor or on stairs
2 Wipe up spills immediately
3 Do not over-polish floors and avoid frayed rugs and carpets
4 Ensure that stairs are well lit with a two-way switch

Children

1 Keep plastic bags, medicines, cleaning agents and other dangerous chemicals out of reach
2 Use short coiled flexes on electrical appliances
3 Fit window locks and stair gates
4 Ensure that babies are strapped securely into high chairs and buggies

Fire Drill

In the event of a fire:
1 Keep calm. Call the fire brigade
2 Ensure that everyone leaves the house by the quickest route. Close doors on the way out to prevent the fire from spreading
3 Do not stop to collect valuables
4 Do not re-enter the house

For small fires:
1 Use a fire blanket or fire extinguisher to quench the fire
2 Never use water on electrical items or burning oil

Hazard symbols

Cleaning agents and household chemicals carry hazard symbols and safety warnings to protect users. Always follow instructions carefully.

Highly flammable

Harmful; irritant

Environmentally damaging

Corrosive – can eat into body tissues

Explosive

Toxic

First aid

First aid is the first treatment given to a person who has been injured or suddenly taken ill before the arrival of an ambulance or qualified medical expert. The aims of first aid are to:
1 **Preserve** life
2 **Prevent** the condition worsening
3 **Promote** recovery

First aid kit

Every home should have a well-stocked first aid kit. This should be kept in a convenient place, out of the reach of children. The following items should be included in a first aid kit:

- Antiseptic lotion or cream
- Thermometer
- Safety pins
- Tweezers
- Sterile gauze
- Adhesive plasters
- Crepe bandages
- Eye bath
- Cotton wool
- Scissors

Simple first aid

Minor burns and scalds

- Make the injured person comfortable
- Pour cold liquid on the injury for 10 minutes
- Remove any clothing or jewellery from the affected area
- Cover the burn and surrounding area with a sterile dressing
- Do not burst blisters or apply lotions, fat or ointments to the injury. Do not use adhesive dressings

Severe burns and scalds

- Lay the injured person down and protect the burned area from contact with the ground
- Pour cold water over the burned area
- Gently remove any rings, watches, belts or shoes from the injured area
- Cover the injury with a sterile dressing
- Do not burst blisters, apply lotions, ointments, fat or adhesive tape to the injury

Shock

- Raise victim's legs as high as possible and support them
- Treat any cause of shock such as bleeding
- Loosen tight clothing
- Do not allow the victim to move, eat or drink

Choking

Choking is caused by a blockage to the airway.

- Bend the victim over and slap him/her on the back
- If this fails to work, try the abdominal thrust
- If the victim is a baby, lay face down along your forearm and slap between the shoulder blades up to four times

Cuts

- If the cut is dirty, clean it by rinsing lightly under running water
- Pat dry and cover with sterile gauze. Apply an adhesive dressing
- If there is severe bleeding from a cut, cover with a sterile dressing or pad and apply pressure over the wound with your fingers or the palm of your hand

- Raise the wounded part above the level of the heart if possible
- Lay the victim down
- Apply a sterile dressing over any original pad and bandage firmly in place

Falls

A strain (pulled and stretched muscles) or a sprain (torn or damaged ligaments) may be treated by the RICE procedure.

R **R**est the injured part
I Apply **I**ce or a cold compress (ice pack or a cloth soaked in ice water)
C **C**ompress the injury (apply gentle, even pressure)
E **E**levate or raise the injured part

Poisoning

- If a person has swallowed a poisonous substance, take him/her immediately to the casualty department of a hospital
- Bring the container of poison to the hospital to help identify the treatment required
- Never try to make the victim vomit
- If the victim is conscious and the lips are burned, give him/her frequent sips of cold water or milk
- If the victim is unconscious, place him/her in the recovery position and send for an ambulance

The **recovery position** prevents the tongue from blocking the airway and allows liquids to drain from the mouth, reducing the risk of the victim inhaling the stomach contents.

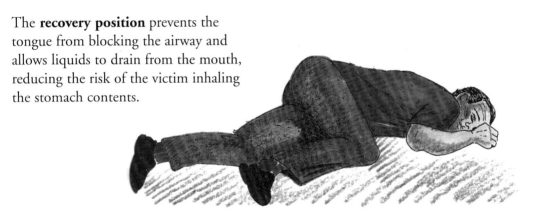

Sample exam questions

Question

1 (a) Give four of the main causes of accidents in the home.
   (b) In relation to each of the causes you have given, suggest one way in which it may be prevented.
   (c) List the items which should be included in a first aid box.
   (d) Where should the first aid box be stored in the home?
   (e) What is meant by a *fire drill*?

(1999, OL)

2 (a) List the safety guidelines which should be followed in order to prevent a fire in the home.
   (b) Name three pieces of fire safety equipment suitable for use in the home.
   (c) Outline the procedure that should be followed to ensure the safety of the occupants of the house in the event of a household fire.
   (d) Describe the first aid treatment for a major burn or scald.
   (e) Explain why water should not be used to extinguish a fire caused by an electrical fault.

(2005, HL)

4.5 Technology in the home

edco home economics REVISE WISE

●●●Learning Objectives

In this chapter you will learn to:

1 Summarise the factors to consider when choosing household appliances
2 Explain how a thermostat works
3 Explain and give examples of the following methods of heat transfer: Conduction, convection and radiation
4 Describe guidelines for the choice, use, care and maintenance of cookers, refrigerators and microwave ovens
5 Describe common features of cookers, refrigerators and microwave ovens
6 Explain star ratings found on refrigerators and frozen foods
7 Differentiate between small electrical appliances with a motor and those with a heating element

Technology has brought huge changes and many improvements in our lives over the last 50 years. Because of technology, running a home today is very different from what it was 50 years ago. The amount of time and labour involved in doing household tasks has decreased considerably.

Points to note

Technology is science used in a practical way in our everyday lives.

Choosing household appliances

When choosing household appliances, consider the following:

1 Cost
2 Energy efficiency
3 Reliability and quality
4 Safety
5 Needs
6 Specifications
7 Design and ease of use
8 Guarantee
9 After sales service

Remember …

… 9 points.

Electric equipment and appliances are examples of household resources. The following large appliances are found in most homes.

Cookers

Cookers may be fuelled by gas or electricity or by a combination of both. Solid fuel and oil-fired ranges are also available.

Modern **gas cookers** include some or all of the following features:

- **Grill:** May be eye level or waist level. Many have a **surface combustion grill** (with small flames over the heating surface to give a larger grilling area)
- **Hob:** There are four **burners** of various sizes
- **Push button ignition** (or may be lit with a **pilot light**)
- **Oven:** Glass-panelled oven door. May have a removable drop-down door and oven roof for easy cleaning
- **Easy-clean oven linings**
- **Oven flame-failure device:** Safety feature to stop the gas flow if the burner goes out
- **Storage area**

Electric cookers may have the following features:

- **Hob:** May consist of four **solid hotplates, coiled rings** or **ceramic** (heat resistant surface)
- Economy **dual rings** may be used for small saucepans
- **Halogen rings** use halogen bulbs fitted under the ceramic hob. They heat up quickly and are very easy to control
- **Grill:** May be used as a small oven. **Dual grill:** Allows one half of the grill to be used for small amounts of food
- **Clock** and **auto-timer:** Oven may be pre-set to switch itself on and off automatically

- **Oven:** Heated by elements at the sides or back. A **fan-assisted oven** heats quickly and cooks evenly. A **thermostat** keeps the oven at the temperature set on the control dial
- **Multifunction ovens:** May be adjusted to suit different cooking conditions, e.g. with or without fan assistance
- **Stay-clean or self-cleaning oven linings**
- Glass-panelled external **oven door**
- **Split-level cookers** may be built into a kitchen. The hob is set into a worktop. The oven is separate and may be built into a unit at eye level or lower

Points to note

How a thermostat works

A thermostat contains a bimetal strip, which is composed of two metals, brass and invar. Brass expands more than invar when heated. When heat is applied, the brass expands and so the strip bends away from the source of electricity. This breaks the electrical circuit and switches off the appliance.

Methods of heat transfer in a cooker

- The hob heats saucepans by **conduction**. The liquid inside the saucepan heats by **convection**
- The grill heats foods by **radiation**
- The oven heats by **convection**

Care and maintenance of cookers

1 Wipe up spills immediately
2 Wipe out the grill pan after use
3 Never drag heavy saucepans across the hob
4 Avoid using harsh abrasive cleaning agents on the surface

5 Use a special cleaner for ceramic hobs
6 When cleaning the cooker:
   (a) Protect your hands, clothes and surroundings
   (b) Use a special caustic oven cleaner to dissolve burnt-in food in the oven
   (c) Wash out, rinse and dry oven
   (d) Wash, dry and polish remaining parts, not forgetting the spill tray under the hob

Choosing a cooker

- The choice between a gas or electric cooker may depend on where you live and the availability of the fuel
- Gas cookers heat quickly and are easily controlled, but are not as clean as electric cookers
- Decide whether or not you want a freestanding cooker or a separate oven and hob
- If choosing an electric cooker, decide on the type of hob you would prefer: ceramic, solid plate or coiled ring

Positioning a cooker

- Position near a gas or electric connection
- Ensure that gas cookers are positioned away from draughts
- Do not place cookers beside a refrigerator or at the end of a line of units

Refrigerators

How to use a refrigerator

- Position away from the cooker or other sources of heat
- Cover food before refrigerating to prevent it from drying out
- Wrap strong-smelling foods
- Never refrigerate apples, bananas or root vegetables
- Never put hot food in the refrigerator
- Do not pack the shelves with food
- Do not open the door unnecessarily
- Store food in the most appropriate position
- When not in use, unplug and leave the door open to allow air to circulate

Points to note

A refrigerator keeps **food cool** by using a special liquid refrigerant, which takes heat from the food and the air inside the refrigerator. The temperature should be between 2°C and 5°C.

Care and maintenance of a refrigerator

1 Defrost regularly as a build-up of ice in the icebox can affect the efficiency of the refrigerator
   - Automatic defrosting: The refrigerator switches off, defrosts and switches on whenever necessary
   - Semi-automatic: Press a button to defrost. When completed, the refrigerator switches itself back on again
2 The inside of the refrigerator should be cleaned with a solution of 1 tbsp bread soda to $\frac{1}{2}$ litre warm water. Rinse and dry. Detergents may flavour the food
3 Wash, dry and polish the outside

Choosing and buying a refrigerator

- Choose one **large enough** to suit the family
- Decide whether you want a **refrigerator** or a **fridge-freezer**

- Ensure that there is enough **space** for it
- Consider how it has to be **defrosted**
- Note the **star rating** on the frozen food compartment

Star rating

The star rating indicates how long frozen food can be stored in the refrigerator icebox or fridge-freezer.

Star Rating	Temperature in Ice Box	Description
*	–6°C	Stores frozen food for one week
* *	–12°C	Stores frozen food for one month
* * *	–18°C	Stores frozen food for three months
|*|* * *|	–18°C to –25°C	Freezes fresh food and stores frozen food for up to one year (fridge-freezer)

Microwave ovens

Microwave ovens cook food very differently to conventional ovens.

Points to note

Microwaves are produced in the oven. These are energy waves which are attracted to water and fat molecules in the food. **They enter the food and cause the food molecules to vibrate, causing friction. This friction produces heat in the food.** This heat is then conducted through the food and the food starts to cook.

Microwave ovens have metal walls. Microwaves reflect off metal, so they bounce off the walls of the oven and enter the food.

Uses of microwave ovens

- Cook food quickly and economically with little loss of nutrients
- Reheat previously cooked foods
- Defrost frozen food quickly

Microwave cookware

- **Glass, paper, plastic** and **china dishes** are **suitable** for use in a microwave oven
- **Metal containers, metal-trimmed dishes, aluminium foil** or **foil-lined covers should not be used** in a microwave oven as they reflect microwaves and can produce sparks which can damage the oven

How to use a microwave oven

- Follow the manufacturer's **instructions**
- The **size, thickness, density** and **volume** of food determine the cooking time
- **Cover** food with a plate, kitchen paper or cling film to prevent it from drying out or soiling the interior of the oven
- **Prod** food with a skin, such as potatoes, tomatoes or egg yolk, to prevent bursting during cooking
- **Arrange** food in a circle, with the thickest part facing outwards, to ensure even cooking
- **Turn** large food items and stir liquids during the cooking process to ensure even distribution of heat
- Allow **standing time**, i.e. leave the food to stand outside of the oven for a few minutes before eating. The food continues to cook in this time
- Wipe up **spillages** immediately
- Do not switch on when **empty** as this can cause damage

Buying a microwave oven

When buying a microwave oven, consider all the points for choosing household appliances (see p. 116) plus the following:

- Some ovens have **turntables**, which ensure more even cooking
- The higher the **wattage**, the more powerful the oven, and the faster it cooks. (Wattage may range from 600W to 1,000W.)

- Ovens may have push-button or dial **controls**
- There are many special features available such as:
  - **Automatic programming** facilities (users can programme in their own settings for a favourite food or recipe)
  - **Temperature probe** (to calculate cooking time)
  - **Auto-weight defrost** (automatically calculates power and time for defrosting)
  - **A browning dish** (to brown foods that are normally grilled or fried)
  - **A browning element** (like a grill)
  - **A child lock**

Small electrical appliances

Small electrical appliances can be divided into two groups:

1 Appliances with a **motor**: These are powered by a small electric motor inside the appliance which drives the moving parts, e.g. food processors, mixers, liquidisers
2 Appliances with a **heating element**: They contain an electric element which heats the food or liquid directly, e.g. toasters, kettles, sandwich toasters

Sample exam questions

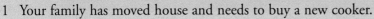

Question

1 Your family has moved house and needs to buy a new cooker.
   (a) What type of cooker would you recommend?
   (b) List the points that should guide you when choosing the cooker.
   (c) Suggest some ways of saving energy when using the cooker.
   (d) Describe how you would clean the cooker.
   (e) Why is good ventilation necessary when cooking?

(2001, OL)

2 A microwave cooker is a popular resource in the modern kitchen.
   (a) Give three advantages of microwave cooking.
   (b) Suggest four different uses of the microwave cooker in food preparation.
   (c) Name three materials suitable for microwave cookware/dishes.
   (d) (i)   List four guidelines for the safe use of a microwave cooker.
        (ii) Explain what is meant by *standing time* in microwave cooking.
   (e) List four important points that should be considered when buying a
        microwave cooker.

(2000, HL)

Your revision notes

4.6 Services to the home

●●●Learning Objectives

In this chapter you will learn to:
1   Summarise the electricity and gas supply to the home
2   Name and state the function of the wires in an electrical appliance
3   State the function of a fuse
4   Recommend guidelines for the safe use of electricity and gas in the home
5   Describe water purification treatments
6   Explain the function of the S-trap or U-bend
7   Explain the following methods of heat transfer: Conduction, convection, radiation
8   Explain what is meant by insulation and give examples of bad conductors of heat (good insulators)
9   Explain what is meant by ventilation and condensation
10 Recommend guidelines for energy efficiency in the home

The main services to the home are electricity, gas and water.

Electricity

All electricity is generated either by water power, wind power, oil, gas, turf or coal. In the home electricity is used for space and water heating, lighting and to run all electrical appliances.

Electricity is transmitted from power stations to homes through the service cable, which is attached to the ESB's **main fuse**. The electricity is then passed through the **meter**, which measures the amount of electricity used in the house. After the meter, wires pass into the **consumer unit** or **fuse box**. From there, wires carry electricity all around the house.

Electrical appliances need at least two wires – a **live wire** to carry electricity to the appliance and a **neutral wire** to return it to the generator. A third **earth wire** may also be present as a safety device. Its function is to convey electric current to the earth if a fault occurs.

Power station ➡ service cable ➡ main fuse ➡ meter ➡ consumer unit

Wire	Colour	Function
Live	Brown	Carries electricity to the appliance
Neutral	Blue	Returns electricity to the generator
Earth	Green & yellow	Conveys electricity to the earth if a fault occurs

A fuse is a safety device. It is a **deliberate weak link** in the electrical circuit. It contains a wire which melts and breaks the circuit if:

- There is an overloading of sockets
- There is overheating of appliances
- A live and neutral wire touch (short circuit)

Wiring a plug

1 Unscrew the central screw and remove the plug top
2 Remove the fuse and loosen the flex clamp screws
3 Loosen the screws of the three terminals – E (earth), L (live) and N (neutral)
4 Carefully cut away 5mm of the outer sheath of the flex and push wire through the flex clamp. Fasten in place
5 Carefully strip enough insulation from the inner sheaths to expose about 6mm of wire and insert wiring under the screw at the correct terminal
6 Tighten screws and ensure there are no stray 'whiskers' of bare wire
7 Fit fuse. Replace cover

Using electricity safely

- Do not overload sockets or adapters
- Use good-quality plugs and appliances
- Never let water come in contact with an electrical appliance
- Replace frayed flexes. Do not attempt to repair them
- Lights and fixed heating appliances in the bathroom should be operated by pull-cord switches
- Never take portable electric appliances into the bathroom

Gas

The two types of domestic gas available in Ireland are **natural gas** and **bottled gas**.

Natural gas is piped ashore from under the seabed off the coast. A branch of the main gas **pipeline** enters the house where the supply is controlled by a **meter control valve**. The gas meter records the amount used in **cubic metres**.

Bottled gas is available in areas which do not receive piped gas.

Gas is used in the home in cookers, heaters and central heating boilers. It is clean and efficient. However, there are some safety precautions that must be followed when using gas.

Safety precautions

- All gas appliances should be **installed** by a qualified person
- Gas cookers, boilers and heaters should be **serviced** regularly
- A good **ventilation** system is essential when using gas appliances as gas uses oxygen when it is burning. This produces fumes, which may be toxic if allowed to build up
- Never block wall **vents**
- **Pilot lights** should be carefully lit
- Gas has a distinctive **smell** so that leaks can be recognised quickly. Never look for gas leaks with a naked flame as gas is flammable and explosive

If you suspect a gas leak ...

1. Open doors and windows
2. Check gas appliances to see if the flame has gone out and if the gas is still on
3. If no appliances have accidentally been left on, turn off the gas at the meter control valve
4. Telephone the gas company emergency number
5. Never ignore the smell
6. Don't smoke or use any naked flames
7. Don't touch light switches or thermostats as they give off a tiny spark when turned on or off
8. Don't use any electrical appliances

Water

Water is used for washing, cooking, heating and sanitation in the home. Fresh water is provided to homes by the local authority (county council or corporation) or by a private group water scheme. Before entering the mains into our homes, it must first be treated to ensure that it is free from impurities.

Water treatment

1. Large objects, such as stones and grit, are removed by **filtering** the water through layers of gravel and sand
2. **Chlorine** is added to destroy harmful bacteria
3. **Fluoride** is added to prevent tooth decay

Filtration ➡ Chlorination ➡ Fluoridation

Water supply

- The water leaves the **reservoir** through a **mains** pipe. A **service pipe** leads from the mains to each house. This supplies water directly to the **cold tap in the kitchen sink**
- A separate pipe fills the **storage tank in the attic** and from there cold water flows to toilets, baths, other sinks in the house, the boiler and hot water cylinder

The kitchen sink

The kitchen sink is usually situated near a window for good light, ventilation and ease of plumbing.

Beneath the sink is an **S-trap** or a **U-bend. This holds water and prevents unpleasant odours and germs from entering the kitchen from the drain.**

Sometimes a sink becomes blocked and water is slow to drain away. To unblock a sink:

1. Remove any pieces of food
2. Block the overflow with a cloth and use a plunger vigorously over the outlet
3. If this fails, put some washing soda crystals down the drain followed by boiling water

4 If this still doesn't work, place a basin under the U-bend and unscrew the nut. Use a piece of wire to loosen the blockage, flush with hot water and replace the nut

Burst pipes

1 Turn off water at the mains
2 Run all cold taps to drain the system

3 Turn off the central heating system. If a back boiler is installed do not light a fire
4 Call a plumber

If pipes have frozen, wrap them in hot rags or thaw using a low setting on a hairdryer. Work backwards from the part of the pipe nearest the tap.

Heating

Heat may be transferred from a heat source in three ways: **conduction, convection** and **radiation**.

Method	Explanation
Conduction	Heat is transferred along a solid object Example: A poker in the fire
Convection	Air or liquid is heated and rises from the heat source. Cool air or liquid replaces it and sets up convection currents Example: Fan heaters
Radiation	Heat rays travel in straight lines and heat the first object they hit Example: Radiant heaters and grills

Insulation

A house can lose 75 per cent of its heat if there is no insulation.

30%

25%–30%

15%

10%

10%–20%

Insulation means **trapping heat in the house by the use of insulating materials**. Good insulating materials are **poor conductors of heat**.

Poor conductors of heat are:
- Still air
- Glass fibre
- Fabrics
- Polystyrene
- Sheep's wool

Forms and uses of insulation

Form	Use
Polystyrene sheets	Cavity walls
Fabrics	Floors (carpets)
Fibreglass, foam pellets, sheep's wool	Attics
Still air	Cavity walls and double-glazed windows
Lagging jackets and factory-insulated sprayed-on coatings	Hot water cylinders

Ventilation

A good ventilation system removes stale air and allows in fresh air without creating a draught.

The **purpose of ventilation** is to:
- Provide fresh air
- Remove stale air
- Control humidity levels
- Prevent condensation
- Control air temperature

Methods of ventilation

- Doors
- Windows
- Room vents
- Fireplaces
- Extractor fans (in kitchens and bathrooms)
- Cooker hoods (in kitchens)

Condensation

Condensation occurs when **warm air comes in contact with a cool surface**. This may lead to dampness, rusting of metals, decay of wood and growth of mould.

Condensation can be controlled by:
- Good ventilation
- Insulation
- An efficient heating system
- Efficient removal of moisture (steam) by the use of vents, windows or extractor fans
- Venting of tumble dryers outside of the house

Lighting

Good lighting is essential in the home as it:
- Prevents eyestrain
- Prevents accidents
- Creates atmosphere in a room
- Provides sufficient light for activities

Energy efficiency tips

1. Choose energy-saving appliances. Look for the energy label
2. Take showers instead of baths
3. Avoid washing under a running tap
4. Switch off lights when not needed
5. Switch off radiators in rooms which are not being used

Remember . . .

REVISE WISE REMEMBER

. . . 10 points.

6   Use a lagging jacket on the hot water cylinder
7   Use energy-saving light bulbs (CFLs)
8   Unplug or switch off TVs and stereos as leaving them on stand-by mode uses electricity
9   Draught-proof your home
10 Use dishwashers and washing machines with a full load only or use economy/half load options

Sample exam questions

Question

1   (a) Sketch and describe the type of sink you would suggest for a kitchen in a modern house.
    (b) Design a work routine for keeping the sink clean and hygienic.
    (c) Outline the procedure you would follow if the sink became blocked.
    (d) Describe one feature of a modern sink.

(1998, OL)

2   Heating and insulation are two important factors to consider in a modern home.
    (a) Name two methods of heat transfer used in home heating and give one example of each.
    (b) Name two fuels which are suitable for home central heating systems.
    (c) (i)   Explain what is meant by insulation.
         (ii) Suggest three areas within the home where good insulation is important.
    (d) Outline briefly how a thermostat works.

(1999, HL)

4.7 Home hygiene

●●●**Learning Objectives**

In this chapter you will learn to:
1 List the guidelines for ensuring a high standard of hygiene in the home and in particular in the kitchen and bathroom
2 List cleaning equipment and common cleaning agents and state their uses in the home
3 Compile a set of guidelines for choosing and buying cleaning agents

Hygiene is the science **concerned with cleanliness** and the maintenance of health.

Bacteria require food, moisture, warmth, air and time to grow and multiply. High standards of hygiene will ensure that these requirements are not available.

Guidelines for home hygiene

- Keep the house **warm and dry** to prevent dampness and fungal growth
- Ensure that the house is **well lit** so that areas in need of cleaning can be seen
- Keep the **drains** clean and free from blockages
- Ensure that the house in **well ventilated**
- Remove unnecessary **clutter** from surfaces
- Wipe up **spillages** immediately

Kitchens

1 Use a bin with a lid. Wash and disinfect weekly
2 Wipe down surfaces before and after preparing food

Remember ...
... 4 points.

3 Change the dishcloth and tea towels every day
4 Keep the sink and draining board clean and tidy

Bathrooms

1 Keep a set of cloths and rubber gloves especially for cleaning the bathroom
2 Keep toilet bowl, seat and flush handle scrupulously clean. Disinfect regularly

Remember ...
... 4 points.

3 Change hand towels, sponges and face cloths daily
4 Avoid toilet seat covers and mats as these hide germs

Equipment

The following equipment is useful in the 'fight against grime':

- Gloves
- Dusters and rags
- Dishcloths
- Sweeping brush
- Mop and bucket
- Vacuum cleaner
- Old toothbrush (for difficult-to-reach spots)
- Paint scrapers or window scrapers

Cleaning agents

Type	Uses
Polishes	Metals, furniture, windows, floors
Detergents	Washing-up liquid, dishwasher detergent, clothes washing detergent
Non-scratch cream cleansers (ceramic hob cleaners)	Sinks, cookers, smooth surfaces
Abrasives, e.g. Brillo, and scouring powders	Stubborn stains on scratch-resistant surfaces
Disinfectants	Sinks, refuse bins, bathroom floors
Bleaches	Stain removal
Water	All purposes – cold to soften dirt and stains, hot to dissolve grease
Oven cleaners	Stubborn stains on oven surfaces and glass doors

- Keep cleaning agents and cleaning equipment together in one cupboard, away from food and cooking utensils
- Polishes and bleaches should be kept out of reach of young children as many household chemicals are poisonous if swallowed

When **choosing and buying cleaning agents**, examine products carefully and consider the following:

1 The cost of the product and the **quantity** it contains
2 Can it be used for **different** cleaning jobs?
3 Can it **harm** or scratch surfaces?
4 Are there any **health risks** in using the product?
5 Does it have clear **instructions** for use?
6 Is it **environmentally friendly**?

Sample exam questions

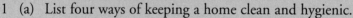

Question

1 (a) List four ways of keeping a home clean and hygienic.
   (b) Give two results of poor hygiene in the kitchen.
   (c) List three rules which should be followed when using a kitchen bin.
   (d) Name two pieces of cleaning equipment you would suggest for use in the home.
   (e) (i) Name one cleaning agent you would use in the kitchen and list the instructions you would follow when using it.
       (ii) Suggest two rules which should be followed when storing cleaning agents.

(2004, OL)

2 A clean hygienic home contributes to healthy living.
   (a) Give four guidelines necessary to ensure a high standard of hygiene in the home.
   (b) List four factors which should be considered when selecting and using household cleaning agents.
   (c) Sketch one hazard symbol to convey that a product is either:
       (i) highly flammable *or* (ii) toxic *or* (iii) harmful and irritant.

(2001, HL)

Your revision notes

4.8 The environment

●●●Learning Objectives

In this chapter you will learn to:
1 List the causes and effects of the following types of pollution: Water, air, noise and litter
2 Explain the following terms: Organic waste, inorganic waste, biodegradable, environmentally friendly
3 Summarise the benefits of recycling and give examples of household waste which can be recycled
4 Compile a list of guidelines for environmentally friendly shopping
5 State the function of the ozone layer and demonstrate your knowledge of how it may be conserved
6 Name organisations concerned with environmental issues

The earth provides many resources such as oil, coal, gas, water, metals and trees. In using the earth's resources, all consumers contribute to the pollution of the environment.

Points to note

Remember: One of our responsibilities as consumers is to use environmental resources carefully.

Pollution

Type	Causes	Effects	What You Can Do
Water	Food production waste, human sewage, animal slurry, silage effluent, oil spills	Dead fish, bad smells, oxygen supply reduced, illness	Choose phosphate-free detergents Use safe garden chemicals Use the correct quantity of fertiliser
Air	Sulphur dioxide, carbon monoxide and smoke, lead from engines, CFC gases	Respiratory diseases, eye irritation, acid rain, climate change	Use natural gas and smokeless coal Choose energy-efficient appliances Buy pump-action sprays rather than aerosols

Type	Causes	Effects	What You Can Do
Noise	Factories, transport, loud music	Depression, anxiety, irritation, insomnia	Choose products with lower noise emissions
Litter	Careless disposal of waste	Destruction of towns, cities and countryside, negative impact on tourism, negative impact on physical and mental health	Dispose of waste carefully Make use of recycling facilities Avoid unnecessary packaging Don't litter and don't tolerate those who do

Waste

Each year we throw away millions of tonnes of waste. Much of our household waste is disposed of by local authorities or private companies.

- **Organic waste**, e.g. food waste, paper and sewage, can be broken down.
- **Inorganic waste**, e.g. plastic, metal and glass, cannot be broken down easily.
- **Biodegradable waste** can be broken down and made harmless by bacteria or other natural means. All organic waste is biodegradable.
- **Environmentally friendly methods of waste disposal** do not harm the environment.

The following may be **recycled**:

- **Metals:** Old metal appliances and aluminium cans
- **Glass:** Bottle banks are available for all types of glass
- **Paper:** Magazines, newspapers, cardboard, office waste
- **Oil:** Used engine and lubricating oils
- **Plastics:** Farmyard plastics, e.g. silage coverings
- **Clothes and rags:** Collected by charity organisations and used in upholstery stuffing
- **Batteries and mobile phones**

Recycling has many **benefits**. It saves on:

- Waste disposal costs
- The need for landfill sites
- Raw materials
- Import bills
- Energy
- Trees

It also:

- Reduces litter
- Creates jobs

Guidelines for environmentally friendly shopping

1 Buy **loose** goods whenever possible
2 Buy **in bulk** where possible
3 Buy products which are **CFC free**
4 Buy products which use **recycled material** in their packaging
5 Bring a **reusable** shopping bag
6 Do not buy **overpackaged** goods

Remember ...

... 10 points.

REVISE WISE REMEMBER

7   Buy **concentrated** products, such as detergents and fabric conditioners, as they use less packaging
8   Choose products which come in **refillable** containers, e.g. cosmetics
9   Choose **energy-saving** appliances
10 **Walk** to the shop!

The ozone layer

The ozone layer (O_3) is located high in the atmosphere. Its function is to absorb harmful ultraviolet rays of the sun and to prevent serious damage to life on earth.

Ultraviolet rays can have serious effects such as:
- Skin cancers
- Cataracts and eye disorders
- Reduction in the yield of certain plants
- Damage to marine life and building materials

Play your part in saving the ozone layer

- Use non-aerosol products such as pump-action sprays or roll-on deodorants
- Choose only ozone-friendly aerosol sprays
- Choose products, e.g. meat, eggs and fast foods, packaged in cardboard or other CFC-free containers
- When replacing old refrigerators or air conditioners, look into arrangements for the recycling of CFCs in the old equipment

Environmental organisations

The following organisations are concerned with environmental issues:
- Greenpeace
- ENFO
- Environmental Protection Agency
- Green schools
- An Taisce
- Green Party

Sample exam questions

Question

1   (a) Give two reasons why it is important to protect the environment.
    (b) Describe four ways in which the environment is being polluted.
    (c) This symbol is often found on packaging materials. What does it mean?

    (d) List six items of household waste which could be recycled.
    (e) Suggest two ways you can help the environment when shopping.

(2000, OL)

2   Over the past few decades many environmental problems such as air and water pollution have increased.
    (a) Give two causes and two effects of (i) air pollution and (ii) water pollution.
    (b) What is the function of the ozone layer?
    (c) Explain (i) organic waste and (ii) inorganic waste. Give two examples of each.
    (d) List four guidelines which should be followed when disposing of household waste.

(1999, HL)

5.1 Household textiles

●●●**Learning Objectives**

In this chapter you will learn to:
1 List the uses of textiles
2 Identify desirable properties of household textiles
3 Compile a list of guidelines for choosing soft furnishings
4 Outline the functions of soft furnishings
5 Suggest suitable textiles for soft furnishings and upholstery

Uses of textiles

Textiles are used for:
- Soft furnishings
- Carpets
- Upholstery
- Bed linen
- Towels
- Table linen

Properties of textiles

A property is a characteristic or quality of a textile. A property can be **desirable** or **undesirable** depending on **the use of the textile.**

Examples of properties are:
- Warm
- Strong
- Non-flammable
- Absorbent
- Stain resistant
- Hardwearing
- Comfortable
- Soft
- Waterproof
- Stretchy
- Washable
- Resilient (bounces back when crushed)
- Crease resistant
- Transparent (lets light through)
- Insulating

Soft furnishings

Soft furnishings include:
- Blinds
- Curtains
- Cushions
- Rugs
- Bedclothes
- Lampshades

Functions of soft furnishings

- Create comfort
- Look attractive
- Express our taste and style

Choosing soft furnishings

When choosing soft furnishings consider the following:
- **Function:** No matter how attractive an item is, it is useless if it does not serve its purpose
- **Attractiveness:** Consider the colour, pattern and texture (feel) of the item
- **Cleaning:** Soft furnishing might require washing, dry cleaning or vacuum cleaning

- **Durability:** Hard wearing items will last a long time
- **Cost:** Choose items which suit your budget

Curtains

Functions of curtains

- Give privacy
- Keep out light
- Keep out sound
- Keep in heat (insulation)
- Reduce draughts
- Look attractive

Desirable properties in curtain fabric

Curtains should:

- Hang/drape well
- Be washable or dry cleanable
- Be pre-shrunk (so that they will not shrink when washed)
- Be closely woven (so that they will keep out light)
- Be resistant to fading
- Be fire resistant

Textiles used in curtains

- Cotton
- Dralon
- Polyester
- Linen
- Wool

Carpets

Desirable properties in carpets

Carpets should be:

- Resilient
- Warm
- Hardwearing
- Fire resistant
- Moth proof

Textiles used in carpets

- Wool
- Nylon
- Acrylic

Upholstery

Desirable properties in upholstery fabric

Upholstery fabrics should be:

- Hard wearing
- Easy to clean
- Stain resistant
- Closely woven
- Comply with fire safety regulations

Textiles used in upholstery

- Heavy cotton
- Wool
- Leather
- Linen
- Velvet
- Dralon

Bed linen

Desirable properties in bed linen

Sheets, pillowcases and duvet covers should be:

- Absorbent
- Smooth
- Comfortable
- Washable
- Crease resistant
- Easily dried

Duvets and blankets should be:

- Warm
- Hard wearing
- Easy to wash
- Lightweight

Textiles used in bed linen

Sheets, pillowcases and duvet covers

- Cotton
- Blends of cotton and polyester
- Flannelette (brushed cotton)
- Linen

Blankets

- Wool
- Wool/nylon blends
- Acrylic

Points to note

The warmth of a duvet is measured by **tog rating**. The least warm is a tog value of 4.5 and the warmest is a tog value of 15.

Sample exam question

Question

(a) Discuss the factors which should be considered when choosing soft furnishings for the home.

(b) Give four functions of curtains.

(c) List three desirable properties of textiles suitable for curtains.

(d) Name two soft furnishings, other than curtains, which you consider suitable for a living room.

(e) (i) Explain what is meant by a fabric finish.

    (ii) Suggest two fabric finishes which could be applied to textiles for use in soft furnishings.

(2003, HL)

●●●Learning Objectives

In this chapter you will learn to:
1 Name natural and manufactured fibres
2 Outline the stages in the production of fibres
3 Describe methods of making yarns and fabrics
4 List the advantages and disadvantages of different kind of fabrics
5 Describe methods of applying pattern and texture to fabrics
6 List the purpose and use of various fabric finishes

Marino Branch
Brainse Marglann Mhuirine
336297

Fibres

Fibres form the basic part of any fabric. **Fibres** are used to **make yarn** and **yarn** is used to **make fabric**.

Classifying fibres

- **Natural fibres** come from plants or animals
- **Manufactured fibres** are created from a mixture of raw materials
- **Regenerated fibres** are manufactured fibres which are made from natural substances such as cellulose
- **Synthetic fibres** are manufactured fibres made from mixtures of chemicals

Stages in the production of fibres

Natural fibres

Cotton

1 The bolls (seed heads) are **picked** from the **cotton plant**
2 The fibres are **separated**
3 They are **pressed** into bales
4 The cotton is **graded**
5 The fibres are **combed**
6 They are **spun** into yarn

PURE COTTON

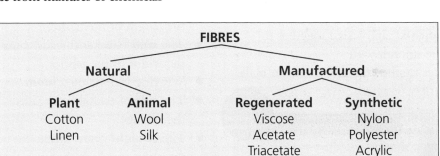

FIBRES			
Natural		**Manufactured**	
Plant	**Animal**	**Regenerated**	**Synthetic**
Cotton	Wool	Viscose	Nylon
Linen	Silk	Acetate	Polyester
		Triacetate	Acrylic
			Elastane

Linen

1 The stems of the **flax plant** are left to **soak** until they rot
2 The fibres are **separated** from the woody parts
3 The fibres are **combed**
4 They are **spun** into yarn

Wool

1 The **fleece** (hair) is removed from the **sheep**
2 The fleece is **graded**
3 It is **cleaned** and **carded** (combed)
4 It is then **spun** into yarn

CERTIFICATION TRADE MARK

WOOLMARK

Silk

1 **Silk worms** feed on the leaves of the **mulberry tree**
2 The worms spin **cocoons** of silk
3 The cocoons are **heated** and **soaked** and the threads are removed
4 The threads are then wound onto **reels**
5 The threads are **spun** into thicker yarn

Manufactured fibres

1 A thick **liquid** is made from raw materials
2 The liquid is forced through tiny holes in a **spinneret**
3 The **filaments** (fibres) become solid
4 Long uniform fibres (**continuous filaments**) are twisted together to make smooth yarn
5 Fibres can be **crimped** or **cut** to make a variety of yarns

Points to note

The term **denier** describes the thickness of manufactured fibres. The lower the number, the finer the yarn.

Fabric construction

Making yarn

- **Spinning** is the process of **twisting fibres into yarn**.
- When two yarns are twisted together, the yarn is called **two ply**. Three yarns make a **three ply** and so on.

Textured yarns

Texture is created in yarns by:

- **Crimping** which makes fabric stretchy
- **Looping** which is used in towelling
- **Knotting** which creates a rough texture
- **Mixing** various yarns and fibres

Methods of making fabrics

There are three basic methods of making fabrics:

1 **Weaving:** Yarns are interlaced at right angles to each other
2 **Knitting:** Loops of yarn are linked together into knots called stitches
3 **Making fabrics without yarns:** In non-woven (bonded) fabrics the fibres are directly stuck together using adhesive, heat, pressure or stitching

Weaving

- Woven fabric has two types of yarn: warp and weft
- The **warp** (strong threads) runs down the length of the fabric
- The **weft** (weaker threads) runs across the width of the fabric
- Weaving is done on a **loom**
- The side of the fabric is called the **selvage**
- The **straight grain** means the direction in which the warp threads run in a fabric

- **Bias** is the diagonal line of a fabric. The fabric stretches when it is pulled along this line

Advantages and disadvantages of different kind of fabrics

Type of Fabric	Advantages	Disadvantages
Woven fabrics	• Easy to sew • Hang well, e.g. in curtains	• Usually not stretchy • Uneconomical to use as the warp threads (straight grain) must run down the length of items such as curtains and patterns must be laid out in one direction only which requires extra fabric
Knitted fabrics	• Stretchy • Warm • Comfortable • Crease resistant	• Difficult to sew • Fray easily • Garments can lose shape
Non-woven fabrics	• Do not fray • Cheap to produce • Keep shape well • Economical to use because there is no straight grain and patterns may be laid out in any direction to make maximum use of fabric	• Do not wear well • Felt is damaged by water • Non-woven blankets do not trap air and therefore are not as warm as wool

Applying pattern to fabric

1 **Dyeing:** A dye is a substance added to fabric to give it colour. Dyeing can be used to apply pattern, e.g. in **tie-dyeing**

2 **Printing:** Applying colour and pattern to one side of the fabric only. Example: Screen printing

3 **Arrangement of yarns** (in woven and knitted fabrics) and **fibres** (in non-woven fabrics) in various ways to produce patterns

Applying texture to fabric

1 Different kind of yarns can be woven together
2 Synthetic fibres create shiny and metallic effects
3 Textured yarns produce textured fabrics

Identifying fibres

Fibres are burnt in a **burn test** so that they can be identified by:
- The way they burn
- Their smell
- The residue

Fabric finishes

A **fabric finish** is a process which **improves the appearance or properties** of a fabric.

Finish	Purpose	Uses
Brushing	Makes fabric feel softer and warmer, e.g. brushed nylon or cotton (flannelette)	Children's nightwear and bed clothes
Polishing (mercerising)	Makes fabric stronger and smoother	Cotton sewing thread, furnishing fabrics
Flame-retarding (Antiflam)	Makes fabric less flammable	Children's nightwear, furnishing fabrics
Stiffening (Trubenising)	Stiffens fabric	Collars and cuffs
Pernament pleating (Koratron)	Pleats don't fall out, no need to iron	Skirts, trousers
Water repelling (Scotchguard)	Stops water soaking into fabric	Coats, jackets
Waterproofing (Scotchguard, Gore-Tex®)	Prevents any water from getting through fabric	Raincoats, outdoor sportswear
Stain repellent (Scotchguard)	Prevents stains from penetrating	Carpets, upholstery, clothing fabrics
Non-shrink (Sanforised)	Prevents shrinking	Furnishing fabrics and clothing
Moth proof	Protects from moths	Clothing, carpets, furnishings
Crease resistance (easy care)	Creases fall out more easily, less ironing required	Shirts, dresses, trousers, tablecloths, curtains
Anti-static (Antistat)	Prevents static which causes shocks and produces clinging	Carpets, clothing

Sample exam question

Question

Cotton is a very versatile and popular textile.
(a) Outline the stages involved in the production of cotton.
(b) List three examples of cotton fabric.
(c) Suggest three fabric finishes which can be applied to cotton.
(d) State two desirable properties of cotton as a household textile.
(e) Sketch the symbol which indicates that a fabric is pure cotton.

(2002, HL)

Your revision notes

5.3 Clothes

●●●**Learning Objectives**

In this chapter you will learn to:
1 List the functions of clothes
2 Compile a list of guidelines for buying clothes
3 Outline factors which influence fashion
4 Explain fashion terms
5 List the points to consider when designing an outfit

Function of clothes

1 Protection from weather, e.g. raincoat
2 Identification, e.g. school uniform
3 Safety, e.g. fire fighter's outfit, chef's outfit, cyclist's padded outfit
4 Expression, e.g. celebration, mourning, formal wear, casual wear
5 Modesty, e.g. swimwear

Guidelines for buying clothes

- Consider the **function** or occasion
- Check the **fit** of each garment
- Consider the current **fashion**
- Check the **care** label
- Consider the **cost**
- Consider the **durability** of the garment
- Consider the **style** of each garment

Accessories

Accessories are extra items worn to complete a look.

The **functions** of accessories are to:
- Create an interesting look
- Change the look of an outfit
- Express our taste and style

Fashion

- Being **in fashion** means having the latest style of clothes, music, cars, furniture, hobbies or toys
- Fashion changes are called **fashion trends**
- A **fashion fad** is a very short-lived fashion

Influences on fashion trends

The following factors influence fashion trends:
1 Famous people
2 The media
3 Historical events
4 The fashion industry
5 Street fashion (everyday clothes which become fashionable)

The fashion industry

- Fashion designers are called **couturiers**
- **Haute couture** (high fashion) means original and very expensive clothes made by fashion designers for individual people
- **Prêt-à-porter** means ready-to-wear clothes
- **Off-the-peg** clothing is affordable clothing which is made using cheaper fabrics and faster production methods

Designing an outfit

The following points should be considered when designing an outfit:

1 Cost
2 Fashion
3 Occasion
4 Comfort
5 Colour
6 Size
7 Design

- **Sketches** are used to show ideas for outfits and accessories
- **Diagrams** must be fully labelled
- A **description** of the outfit must also be written

Points to note

Line is a feature of design:
- Vertical lines add height and make a person look slimmer
- Horizontal lines make a person look broader
- Curved lines give a soft look to clothes
- Diagonal lines are dramatic and striking

Sample exam questions

Question

You have been asked to design an outfit suitable for leisure wear.
(a) List the points you would consider when designing the outfit.
(b) Sketch and describe the outfit you would design.
(c) Suggest suitable fabric(s) for the outfit and give reasons for your choice.
(d) Describe one method you could use to personalise the outfit you have designed.
(e) What factors influence fashion trends?

(2004, HL)

5.4 Needlework skills

●●●**Learning Objectives**

In this chapter you will learn to:
1 List essential items of sewing equipment
2 Compile a list of guidelines for selecting fabric for sewing
3 List guidelines for buying and using a sewing machine
4 Name the parts of the sewing machine
5 Show the correct method of threading a sewing machine
6 Name the various hand and machine stitches and state their functions
7 Describe the methods used to finish flat seams
8 Sketch a household item and describe the stages to follow when making
   (a) a garment and (b) a household item

Essential items of sewing equipment

- Scissors
- Needles
- Thimble
- Pins
- Thread
- Measuring tape
- Stitch ripper
- Pinking shears
- Tailor's chalk

Selecting fabric for home sewing

- Fabric should **not fray** much
- Fabric should **not have flaws**
- Fabric should be **non-slip**
- It should be **not too stretchy**
- Check that the **colour** is suitable
- Check that the **weight** of the fabric is suitable

- Work out the **amount** of fabric you need before you shop
- **Avoid** fabric with a nap or one-way designs

Points to note

Some fabrics feel smooth if you rub them one way and rough if you rub them the other way. This is called a **nap**.

One-way designs are patterns which all face the same direction.

Buying a sewing machine

When buying a sewing machine consider the following factors:
- **Cost**
- Type of **stitches** you will need to do
- **Attachments** included with the machine
- **After sales service**
- **Guarantee**

The sewing machine

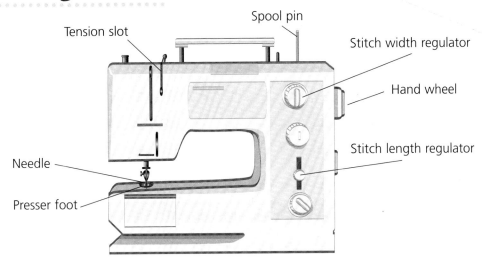

Tension slot

Spool pin

Stitch width regulator

Hand wheel

Stitch length regulator

Needle

Presser foot

Threading the sewing machine

Thread the machine according to the instructions. The following sequence is often used:

1 **Spool pin → thread guide → tension slot → thread guide → take up lever → thread guide → needle**
2 Insert the filled **bobbin**
3 **Turn** the wheel until the needle thread catches the bobbin thread
4 **Pull** both threads towards the back of the machine

Guidelines for using a sewing machine

- **Thread** the machine properly
- **Raise** the needle to its highest position
- **Adjust** the stitch length and tension to suit the fabric
- **Test** the stitch on a scrap of fabric
- **Insert** the fabric from the front and then lower the presser foot
- **Lower** the needle with the hand wheel
- **Press** lightly on the foot pedal
- **Guide** the fabric towards the machine

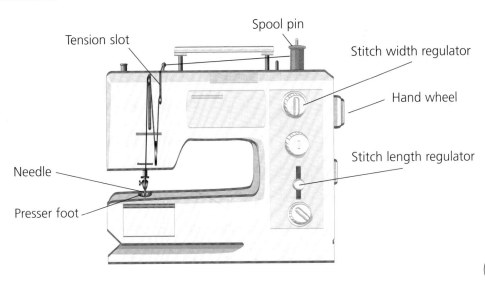

Tension slot

Spool pin

Stitch width regulator

Hand wheel

Stitch length regulator

Needle

Presser foot

- At the **end** of a line, **reverse** for a few stitches
- **Raise** the needle and **lift** the presser foot
- **Pull** the fabric to the back and cut thread

Care of a sewing machine

- Follow the instructions for use and cleaning
- Do not run a threaded machine without fabric
- Cover when not in use to avoid dust
- Oil moving parts occasionally
- Have machine serviced occasionally

Machine faults and possible causes

Machine Fault	Possible Cause
Needle breaks	• Pulling fabric before raising needle • Tension too tight • Needle too fine or inserted incorrectly • Loose presser foot
Thread breaks	• Tension too tight • Incorrect threading of machine • Poor quality thread • Needle inserted incorrectly
Uneven stitches	• Incorrect threading • Needle set too high or too low • Pulling or pushing fabric while machining • Needle blunt or inserted incorrectly
Looped stitches	• Tension too loose • Incorrect threading of machine • Bobbin threaded incorrectly

Machine stitches

Name	Uses
Straight stitch -------------------------------	• Most sewing, e.g. seams, to apply waistbands and to sew hems on non-stretch fabrics • Stitch length can be adjusted • Long stitches are used for thick fabric
Zig-zag stitch /\/\/\/\/\/\/\/\/\/\/\/\	• For finishing seams, sewing on elastic and sewing stretchy fabric

Name	Uses
Blind stitch ....∧....∧....∧....∧....∧....∧....∧....	● For hems and decorative work
Buttonhole stitch	● For making buttonholes
Embroidery stitches 	● Decorative work

Hand stitches

Stitches can be divided into temporary and permanent stitches.

● **Temporary stitches** include tacking, tailor tacking and gathering

● **Permanent stitches** include running, backstitching, hemming, slip hemming and machine stitching

Name	Uses
Tacking (Basting) 	● To hold two pieces of fabric (a hem or seam) in position while being stitched ● To hold a garment together for fitting ● As a guide for machining
Running 	● For seams or for gathering fabric by hand

Name	Uses
Gathering	• To make a wide piece of fabric fit a narrow piece
Backstitching	• A strong stitch that can be used to sew seams instead of machining
Hemming	• To hold small hems, e.g. on facings, bindings, backs of waistbands and collars • Not suitable for hems of clothes
Slip hemming	• For hems of clothes
Tailor tacking	• To transfer pattern markings from a pattern onto fabric

Embroidery

Name of Stitch	Uses
Stem stitch	• To outline
Chain stitch	• To outline • To fill in shapes
Satin stitch	• To fill in shapes
Long and short stitch	• To fill in shapes • To give a shaded effect

Flat seams

- **Seams** are made **when two pieces of fabric are joined by a line of sewing**

- A **flat seam** is sewn with the **right sides** of the fabric **facing each other**

Seam finishes

A flat seam is usually finished using:
1 Straight stitching (edge machining)
2 Zig-zag stitching
3 Pinking shears (to trim the edges of closely woven fabric)

Edge machining (straight stitching)

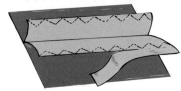

Zig-zag machining

Using pinking shears

Points to note

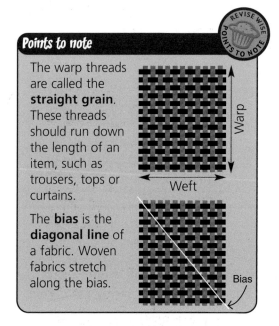

The warp threads are called the **straight grain**. These threads should run down the length of an item, such as trousers, tops or curtains.

The **bias** is the **diagonal line** of a fabric. Woven fabrics stretch along the bias.

Warp

Weft

Bias

Pattern markings

Pattern markings are transferred to fabric using:
1 Tailor tacks
2 Tailor's chalk
3 Tracing wheel and carbon paper

Making a garment

Items needed to make a garment

- Pattern
- Thread
- Tailor's chalk
- Scissors
- Needles
- Pins
- Measuring tape
- Stitch ripper

Stages to follow when making a garment

1 Prepare the pattern
2 Lay the pattern on the fabric
3 Cut out the fabric
4 Transfer the pattern markings
5 Remove the pattern
6 Sew seams:
  (a) Place two pieces of fabric together with **right sides facing** and edges exactly on top of each other. Match notches
  (b) Pin and tack on the fitting line
  (c) Remove pins and machine
  (d) Remove the tacking and **press** the seam open
  (e) Neaten the edges with edge machining
  (f) Turn up hems

Sketch and description of a household item

Name of item: Multipurpose cover

Sketch:

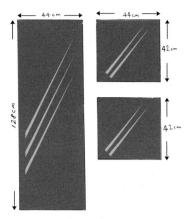

Description: This is a multipurpose fabric cover which can be used to cover items such as a computer, TV or a stack of books. It has been personalised with embroidery.

Type of fabric: Light denim

Reasons for choice:

1 It is easy to sew
2 It is closely woven
3 It is durable

Stages to follow when making the household item

1 Make a **pattern** by cutting out three shapes consisting of one large shape (128cm x 44cm) and two smaller shapes (42cm x 44cm)
2 Lay the **pattern** on single fabric and **cut out** fabric (see top of next column)
3 **Mark the fitting line** all around the edges, using tailor's chalk

4 Turn up a **hem** on the two small pieces along the 42cm edge
5 Turn up a **hem** in the same way on the narrow edges of the large shape
6 **Join** the small pieces to the large piece as follows:
   (a) With right sides together, pin one side piece to the long section, beginning at the hems and working all the way round to the other end
   (b) **Tack** and **machine** along the fitting line
   (c) Repeat with the other side
7 Remove tacking and **finish** the seams using zig-zag sewing
8 **Personalise** and add a decorative finish with **embroidery**.

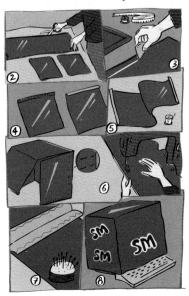

Sample embroidery finish and description

Stitch	Description
Stem stitch 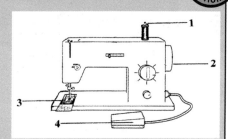	1 First I transferred the design onto the fabric using a tracing wheel and carbon paper 2 I started with a backstitch 3 I made even, slightly slanted stitches along the line, working from right to left 4 The thread was kept at the right of the needle 5 I finished with a back stitch

Sample exam questions

Question

1 (a) Name the parts of the sewing machine labelled 1, 2, 3 and 4.
   (b) List four guidelines which should be followed when using a sewing machine.
   (c) Name each of these machine stitches.
      (i)

      (ii)

   (d) Why is it important to test a machine stitch on a sample of fabric?
   (e) List six items you would expect to find in a sewing box.

   (2004, OL)

2 (a) List four factors which the consumer should consider when buying a sewing machine for use at home.
   (b) List five guidelines which should be followed when using a sewing machine.
   (c) Name two machine stitches and suggest one use for each stitch.
   (d) Suggest one possible cause for each of the following machine faults:
      (i)   Thread breaking
      (ii) Looped stitches
      (iii) Needle breaking

   (2001, HL)

3 (a) Sketch and describe an attractive household item you could make as a house warming gift for your aunt.
   (b) State the fabric(s) you would use and give two reasons for your choice.
   (c) Outline the stages you would follow when making the household item. Use diagrams to illustrate your answer.
   (d) Describe one method you could use to personalise the item.

   (1999, HL)

●●●Learning Objectives

In this chapter you will learn to:
1 Compile a list of guidelines for taking care of clothes
2 Explain care labels
3 Explain the terms used in fabric care
4 Describe how to remove stains

Guidelines for taking care of clothes

1 Before storing clothes:
  - Remove stains
  - Wash or dry clean
  - Mend
2 Use shaped hangers
3 Fold knitwear and store it flat

International care labelling system

Washing instructions

Washing instructions are indicated by a washtub which shows the recommended temperature and the washing action to be used.

The bar symbol

The bar symbol shows the washing action to be used:
- No bar: Maximum washing action and spin 40°
- Single bar: Medium washing action and short spin 40°
- Broken bar: Minimum washing action 40°

Drying instructions

Dry flat	
Line dry	
Tumble dry	
Drip dry	
Do not tumble dry	

Textile/Machine Code	Machine Wash	Hand Wash	Fabric
95°	Maximum wash in cotton cycle	Hand hot (50°C) or boil. Spin or wring	White cotton and linen articles without special finishes

Ironing instructions

Hot iron

Warm iron

Cool iron

Do not iron

Dry cleaning instructions

Dry clean ⒜ⓅⒻ

Do not dry clean ⊗

Bleaching instructions

Bleach may be used

Do not use bleach

Points to note

An **X** through a symbol means that the treatment should not be carried out.

Fabric care products

Fabric Care Product	Function
Non-biological detergent	Removes dirt
Biological detergent	Contains chemicals called enzymes which break down protein stains
Fabric conditioner	Makes fabric softer
Colour run remover	Removes the unwanted colour when colours run in the wash
Stain remover	Removes stains

Points to note

Colour fast fabrics do not run in the wash.
Biological detergents damage waterproof and flame resistant finishes.

Commercial stain removers

- Follow the **instructions**
- **Test** the stain remover on a hidden part of the garment
- Use in a **well-ventilated** area
- **Do not use near flames**
- **Keep away** from children
- Use **rubber gloves**
- **Wash hands** after use

Removing common stains

- **Remove stain before** it dries into the fabric
- **Scrape** or blot off stain as much as possible
- **Soak** in cold water
- Try **gentle treatment** first
- Use a **commercial stain remover** if necessary

The following **methods** may be used to remove **stains**.

Stain	Method of Removal
Chewing gum	Freeze and scrape off. Wash as usual
Perspiration, tea and coffee	Soak in warm water with a biological detergent. Wash as usual
Blood, gravy and egg	Soak in cold water. Wash with biological detergent
Grass and ink	Soak in methylated spirits. Wash as usual
Chocolate	Dab with glycerine. Wash as usual
Grease	Dab with solvent. Wash as usual

Drying and ironing clothes

- **Spin drying:** Removes most of the water from clothes
- **Tumble drying:** Clothes are tumbled in warm air in the rotating drum of the tumble dryer so that the water evaporates
- **Steam iron:** Steam evaporates at the base of the iron which removes wrinkles more quickly

Ironing guidelines

In general, the required heat settings are:
- **Cool:** Acrylic, nylon and viscose
- **Warm:** Polyester, wool and silk
- **Hot:** Cotton and Linen

Sample exam question

Question

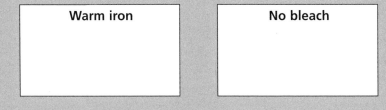

Care Label A	Care Label B
55% Cotton 45% Polyester	50% Wool 50% Acrylic

(a) Using the information on the care labels above, name two man-made fabrics and name two natural fabrics.

(b) Which care label would you expect to find on a school uniform jumper? Give one reason for your answer.

(c) Sketch the symbols for (i) warm iron and (ii) no bleach.

Warm iron	No bleach

(d) Explain the purpose of each of the following in fabric care.
   (i) Detergent
   (ii) Fabric conditioner

(2003, OL)

Examination section

- **The examination paper**

- **Examination tips**

- **Learning tips**

- **Breakdown of topics from previous examinations**

- **Past exam paper with sample answers and marking scheme**

The Junior Certificate Exam is structured as follows:

	Higher Level	Ordinary Level
Food studies (practical)	35%	45%
Project	15%	15%
Written exam	50%	40%

The examination paper

The **written exam** covers the five core areas of the course:

1. Food studies and culinary skills
2. Consumer studies
3. Social and health studies
4. Resource management and home studies
5. Textile studies

The exam paper is laid out in two sections: **Section A** and **Section B**.

Section A

- Section A is worth **80 marks**
- It is composed of **twenty-four short questions**
- **Twenty questions** from this section must be answered on the answer sheet at **Higher Level**
- **Sixteen questions** must be answered at **Ordinary Level**

Section B

- At **Higher Level** Section B is worth **110 marks**
- At **Ordinary Level** Section B is worth **160 marks**
- It is composed of **six questions** out of which you must **answer four**. There are usually a number of subsections to each question and it is important that you attempt every part of the question.
- **Higher Level** students answer this section in a **separate answer book**.
- At **Ordinary Level**, Section A and Section B are contained in **one answer booklet**.

Examination tips

- Revise all sections of the course. Do not leave out any sections
- Plan a revision timetable (see p. 178). Always work with pen and paper and test yourself as you go along
- Work on past exam papers to become familiar with the layout of the paper
- Practise sketching diagrams, menus and consumer letters of complaint
- On the day, follow a time plan. Here is a suggestion:

	Higher Level (2hr 30min)
Read paper and mark questions you will answer	10min
Answer Section A	25min
Four questions from Section B	4 @ 25min = 1hr 40min
Revise answers	15min

	Ordinary Level (2hr)
Read paper and mark questions you will answer	10min
Answer Section A	20min
Four questions from Section B	4 @ 20min = 1hr 20min
Revise answers	10min

- When reading the paper, **tick** the questions you intend to answer and **underline** or highlight the key words, e.g. _List three methods of food preservation and explain how one of the methods you have listed is carried out_.

- When writing your answers, **number** each question and each sub-section, leaving spaces between them. Make sure you **attempt** every part of the question
- If possible, **tabulate** your answer (present in a table) as this is clearer and there is less repetition
- Leave **space** at the end of each question in case you think of anything you may want to add when reading over your answers in the last 10 or 15 minutes
- Keep your writing **legible** and use pencil when drawing clear, well-labelled diagrams
- Ensure you have answered the correct **number** of questions from each section.

Common pitfalls

- Questions are not read carefully, resulting in key parts or diagrams being omitted
- The following terms are often confused or not known: _empty kilocalories, proportion, emphasis, bias, selvage, peristalsis, property, fabric finish, impulse buying, ovulation, foetus_
- The following symbols and diagrams are often confused or not known: _quality symbols, hand sewing stitches, male and female reproductive systems_
- Terms are misinterpreted, e.g. _constituents_ of foods, _factors_ to be considered, _factors_ which contribute
- Answers are vague, unclear, off the point or too short
- Proper menu format is not used when presenting menus
- Terms and phrases used in questions are not understood (see following table for an explanation of the language used in questions)

Language used in questions

Terms and Phrases Used	Requirements
• Name • Give • List • State • Tick • Complete (the table) • Identify • Define	Require short concise answers
• Explain • Suggest • Describe • Discuss • Examine • Summarise • Demonstrate • Classify	More detailed answers required, consisting usually of a number of sentences
• Design • Plan • Sketch • Set out • Illustrate	Menus, diagrams, symbols, room layout, an outfit or a household item
• Differentiate between • Contrast • Distinguish between	Point out the differences between two items
• Compare	Point out the similarities between two items
• Evaluate	Assess the value of something, e.g. the good and bad points
• Comment on • Judge • Recommend	Give your opinion and back it up with accurate and relevant facts

Learning tips

1 **Revise** and **practise labelling** the following **diagrams and symbols**

Study Unit	Diagrams and Symbols
Food studies	• Food pyramid • Digestive system • Structure of an egg • Structure of the wheat grain • Cooking utensils • Gluten-free symbol
Consumer Studies	• Safety symbols • Quality marks
Social and health studies	• Tooth structure • Types of teeth • Skin • Male and female reproductive systems • Respiratory system • Heart structure • Blood vessels
Resource management and home studies	• Double insulated symbol • Recycling symbol • Parts of a cooker • Plug (wiring) • Work triangle • Refrigerator star markings
Textile studies	• Fabric construction (selvage, bias, warp, weft) • Care labels • Stitches (hand sewing and embroidery) • Fibre symbols • Seams • Sewing equipment • Parts of a sewing machine

2 Practise **sketching** the following:
   • Hazard symbols
   • Safety symbols
   • Room plans
   • Care labels
   • A household item
   • A specified outfit

3 Practise **menu layouts** and a consumer **letter of complaint**

4 Ensure you can explain the following terms:
   • Au gratin
   • Sauté

(*continued on next page*)

- Marinade
- Baste
- Al dente
- Standing time (in relation to microwave cookery)
- Table d'hôte
- À la carte
- Empty kilocalories
- Organic

- Biodegradable
- Offal
- Rickets
- Hypervitaminosis
- Peristalsis
- Impulse buying
- PAYE
- PRSI
- Norms
- Ovulation

- Menopause
- Ergonomics
- Upholstery
- Haute couture
- Prêt-à-porter
- Proportion
- Emphasis
- Bias
- Selvage
- Fabric finish

Your revision notes

Breakdown of topics from previous examinations

Junior Certificate Higher Level Questions
(S = short questions; L = long questions)

	2004	2005	2006	2007	2008	2009	2010	2011
Food Studies								
Nutrition	S,S,L	S,S,L	S	S	S,S	S		
Diets	S	S	S,L		S,L	S,S		
Food Safety & Hygiene	S	L		S	S	L		
Meal Planning		L						
Cookery Terms								
Food Preservation & Processing			S	S		L		
Digestion		S						
Starting to Cook				L				
Meat	S					L		
Fish		S		S	L			
Milk & Milk Products		S	L		S	S,S		
Eggs				L	S			
Cereals & Baking	L	S		S				
Vegetables	S		S	L				
Fruit	L							
Soups & Sauces			S		L	S		
Consumer Studies								
Rights & Responsibilities			S	L				
Protection	L	S	S	S,L	S,S	L		
Money Management	S,S	S,S		S,S	L			
Quality		S			S	S		
Advertising		L			S			
Shopping	S,S		S,L			S,S		➡

	2004	2005	2006	2007	2008	2009	2010	2011
Social & Health Studies								
The Family	S	L						
Roles & Relationships			S,S	S				
Adolescence					S	S		
Health								
Health Hazards	S	S		S	S	S		
Reproduction	S	S	S	L	S	S		
Skin					L			
Circulatory System	L		S	S		L		
Respiratory System		S		S				
Teeth	S		L		S	S		
Resource Management & Home Studies								
Management								
Design	L		S,S,S	S	L	S		
Safety & First Aid		L		S	S			
Technology in the Home	S,S			L		S,L		
Services to the Home	S,S	S	S,L	S		S		
Home Hygiene								
Community					S			
Environment		S	S	S	S,S,S,	S,S		
Textile Studies								
Textiles		S,S			S	L		
Fashion & Design	S,L		S	S,L	S,S	S		
Needlework Skills		S,S	S	S	S,S	S,S		
Textile Care	S	S,S	S	S	S	S,L		
Sewing Machine	S	S	L			S		
Fibres & Fabrics	S,S	L	S,S	S,S	L	S		

Past exam paper
with sample answers and marking scheme

Section A   80 marks

(80)

Answer 20 (twenty) of the following questions. All questions carry equal marks.

1. List **four** healthy eating guidelines.   4

    (i)   *Eat less sugar/Drink more water*

    (ii) *Eat less fat/Have a balanced diet*

    (iii) *Eat less salt/Reduce alcohol consumption*

    (iv) *Eat more fibre rich foods etc.*

2. Outline **two** reasons why a teenager may become a vegetarian.   4

    (i)   *May object to killing animals*

          May believe that it is a healthier diet

    (ii) *May dislike the taste of meat*

3. Give **two** effects of cooking on fish.   4

    (i)   *The protein coagulates and shrinks/Fish flesh becomes opaque/Loss of Vit B*

    (ii) *Microorganisms are destroyed/Connective tissue dissolves/Breaks apart easily*

4. Name **two** different classifications of cheese and give **one** example of **each** class. 4

Classification of Cheese	Example
(i) *Soft*	(i) *Cottage/Brie/Camembert*
(ii) *Semi-hard/Semi-soft*	(ii) *Edam/Gouda/Stilton*
Hard	*Cheddar/Cheshire/Parmesan*
Processed	*Cheese strings/Cheese spreads/Slices*

(165)

5. Explain **each** of the following: 4

   (i) **Rickets** – *Bone disease found in children suffering from a lack of Vitamin D or Calcium*

   (ii) **Hypervitaminosis** – *An excess of Vit A or Vit D in the diet which is harmful to the body*

6. Name **one** different type of flour that matches **each** of the following descriptions: 4

Description	Type of Flour
(i) contains the outer husk and bran	(i) *Wholegrain/wholemeal*
(ii) contains extra gluten	(ii) *Strong flour*
(iii) suitable for coeliacs	(iii) *Gluten free flour/rice flour/cornflour*
(iv) raising agent has been added	(iv) *Self-raising flour*

7. What is the function of the office of the Ombudsman? 4
   Deals with complaints about government agencies or public services, e.g. Health Boards, An Post

8. Explain the difference between gross income and net income. 4
   Gross income is the amount of money earned. Net income is the 'take home pay' after deductions have been taken from Gross income.

9. Give **two** features of a good quality service. 4
   (i) *The person carrying out the service should be skilled/ friendly/efficient.*

   Good quality materials should be used.

   (ii) *The work should be guaranteed for a period of time.*

10. Explain **each** of the following: 4
    (i) **PAYE** – *Pay As You Earn. Income Tax deducted from Gross income which is used by the government to run the country*

    (ii) **PRSI** – *Pay Related Social Insurance. Money deducted from Gross income which the government uses to fund unemployment benefits/maternity leave/ illness etc.*

11. Name the parts of the digestive system labelled **1**, **2**, **3** and **4**. 4

    1. *Liver*

    2. *Stomach*

    3. *Large intestine*

    4. *Anus*

12. Give **two** effects of alcohol abuse on society. 4

    (i) *Increase in crime rate/Increase in road accidents and deaths/ Absenteeism from work*

    (ii) *Cost to state treating alcohol related illnesses*

13. Explain **each** of the following terms in relation to the female reproductive system: 4

    (i) **Ovulation** – *An egg is released from the ovary into the fallopian tube. Occurs in the middle of the menstrual cycle/periods*

    (ii) **Menopause** – *This occurs to women usually between 45 and 55 (Middle aged) when their menstrual cycles/periods cease.*

14. Give **two** functions of the lungs. 4

    (i) *Take in Oxygen/Release Carbon Dioxide*

    (ii) *Release small amounts of water vapour*

15. Outline **two** safety precautions which should be taken when using
    electricity in the home.   4

    (i) *Do not overload sockets/Avoid using adaptors*

    (ii) *Avoid trailing flexes/Do not allow contact with water*

16. Suggest **two** different types of accommodation suitable for a student
    living away from home.   4

    (i) *Rented flat or apartment/Rented house sharing with others*

    (ii) *Rented bed-sitter/Stay with family in 'digs'*

17. List **four** soft furnishings used in the home.   4

    (i) *Curtains*   (ii) *Cushions*

    (iii) *Rugs/Mats*   (iv) *Bedlinen/Throws etc.*

18. Explain the term *inorganic waste – Waste that is not bio-degradable,
    i.e it will not break down over time*   4

    Give **one** example of *inorganic waste – Glass/Plastic/Metal*

19. Explain how **each** of the following stains may be removed from a cotton jersey: 4

    (i) **Grass** *– Dab with methylated spirits and then wash as normal.*

    (ii) **Blood** *– If the stain is fresh, soak in cold water and then wash.
    If the stain is old, soak in warm water and enzyme detergent.*

20. Give **two** reasons why the thread may break when using a sewing machine.   4

    (i) *Needle incorrectly inserted*

    Top tension too tight

    (ii) *Incorrect threading*

    Poor quality thread

21. Name **two** embroidery stitches and suggest a different use for **each** one.   4

Embroidery Stitch	**Use**
(i) *(a) Satin stitch (b) Stem stitch*	(i) *(a) To fill in shapes*
	(b) To outline, e.g. initials
(ii) *(a) Chain stitch (b) Long and Short*	(ii) *(a) As an outline*
	(b) To fill in wide designs

22. Explain what **each** of the following fabric care symbols indicate.   4

Drip dry/Dry flat

Very hot wash – Suitable for white cotton

95°

23. Give **two** desirable properties of **each** of the following textile items: 4

Winter jacket   (i) *Warm/Stain resistant/Waterproof*

(ii) *Durable/Insulating etc.*

Bed sheets   (i) *Washable/Smooth*

(ii) *Light weight etc.*

24. Name **two** methods of transferring pattern markings to fabric.   4

(i) *Tailor tacks/Tailor's chalk*

(ii) *Carbon paper/Tracing wheel*

Section B   220 marks

Q1

55

1. Porridge is a healthy, wholesome breakfast cereal.
   The following information is displayed on a packet of porridge oatflakes.

PORRIDGE OATFLAKES

Nutritional Information		**Cooking Methods**
Per 30g serving		**Method A:** Add one cup of oatflakes to three cups of milk.
Energy	465kJ/110kcal	Boil and stir for 4–5 minutes.
Protein	3.3g	**OR**
Carbohydrate	19.8g	**Method B:** Add $\frac{1}{3}$ cup of oatflakes to $\frac{2}{3}$
(of which sugars)	0.3g	cup of water. Stir and place in a bowl in a
Fat	1.5g	microwave oven.
(of which saturates)	0.3g	Cook for 2–3 minutes.
Fibre	2.7g	Note – cooking times may vary according
Sodium	0.003g	to microwave rating.

(a) From the information given above:

   (i)   evaluate the nutritive value of porridge oatflakes;   = 5 x 3   15
         Expect reference to 5 nutrients listed
         Name each nutrient and state the no. of g. in each
         State whether porridge is high or low in each nutrient

   (ii) name **two** nutrients which are not present in porridge
         oatflakes and suggest **one** way of including **each** of
         the nutrients you have named in the diet;   = (2 x 3) x 2   12
         Vit C – Drink orange juice   Iron – Eat liver
         Calcium – Drink milk   Vit B – Eat cereals

   (iii) state which cooking method, **A** or **B**, you would
         choose when making porridge and give **two** reasons
         for your choice.
                              Cooking method = 1; Reasons = 2 x 2   5
         A *– Contains milk which adds calcium, easy to cook on hob*
         B *– Less calories, less washing up, quicker*

(b) Give **three** reasons why breakfast is an essential meal for
school-going teenagers. = 3 x 3 — 9
Raises blood sugar levels/ Helps concentration/ Prevents headaches and tiredness/
Results in more efficient work/ Aids the prevention of accidents

(c) Design a balanced breakfast menu, to include porridge,
suitable for a school-going teenager. = 5 x 2 — 10
Must include porridge = 2 marks; must be balanced = 2 marks;
must have menu format = 2 marks
Accept any other 2 points @ 2 marks each
Include fruit or fruit juice, include dairy group,
include bread or toast, include coffee or tea or juice

(d) Explain what is meant by *'cooking times may vary according to*
microwave rating'. — 4
Microwave cookers are classified/rated according to their power.
The higher the power, the quicker the cooking time,
e.g. 900W is quicker than 650W.

Q2 ⬤⬤⬤⬤ (55)

2. (a) Outline the conditions that favour the growth
of microorganisms. = 4 x 3 — 12
 • *Moisture*
 • *Warmth*
 • *Food*
 • *pH*
 • *Oxygen*

(b) (i) Name **one** food poisoning bacterium. = 1 x 3
Salmonella, Staphylococci, Clostridia, Listeria
 (ii) Give **two** possible sources of this bacterium. = 2 x 3 — 9
 • *Salmonella – poultry, eggs, pets, insects, intestines*
 • *Staphylococci – cuts, nose, mouth, throat*
 • *Clostridia – intestines of humans, birds, animals*

(c) List **three** symptoms of food poisoning. = 3 x 3 — 9
Nausea, Vomiting, Diarrhoea, Fever, Abdominal pain/cramp

(d) Give **three** advantages of preserving food. = 3 x 3 — 9
 • *Prevents waste, saves money*
 • *Seasonal foods are available all year round*
 • *Adds variety to the diet*
 • *Saves time and labour as food has been prepared*
 • *Food can be transported easier*

(e) List **three** methods of food preservation and explain
how **one** of the methods you have listed is carried out.

Expect 3 methods @ 4 marks each = 12

Expect 1 explanation @ 4 marks = 4

16

- *Canning – high temperatures, airtight cans*
- *Freezing – very low temperatures, water changes to ice*
- *Drying – moisture is removed*
- *Freeze drying – food is frozen, then moisture is removed*
- *Irradiation – energy waves are passed through the food to kill microbes*
- *Jam making – fruit is boiled, high sugar content, airtight jars*
- *Pasteurisation – milk is heated and cooled rapidly to kill harmful bacteria*
- *Bottling – very high temperature, sterilised and airtight glass bottle*

Q3
● ● ● ●

55

3. (a) List **four** sources of advertising.   = 4 x 3   12

- *Newspapers/magazines*
- *Concerts/internet*
- *Television/radio*
- *Buses/trains/bus shelters*
- *Cinema/DVDs*
- *Labels/logos on clothing*
- *Billboards/sporting events*
- *Carrier bags/shop windows/leaflets*

(b) Give **three** advantages and **three** disadvantages
of advertising.   = (3 x 3) x 2   18

Advantages
- *Provides information*
- *Employs many people*
- *Increases sales*
- *Keeps down the cost of magazines and newspapers*
- *Launches new products*

Disadvantages
- *Increases the cost of products*
- *May mislead the consumer*
- *Can reinforce stereotypes*
- *Can affect the natural surroundings*
- *May result in overspending*

(c) (i) Describe **three** marketing techniques used
in supermarkets. = 3 x 4 12
- *Luxuries placed at eye level*
- *Sweets beside the checkout*
- *Essentials at back of shop*
- *Items positioned by association*
- *Three for two offers*
- *Slow background music*
- *Samples of new products*
- *Loss leader technique*

(ii) Name the marketing technique you think is Name = 2 6
most effective **and** give a reason for your answer. Reason = 4
Expect one marketing technique described with a
valid reason/own opinion.

(d) Outline the role of the Advertising Standards Authority of Ireland. 7
Voluntary body that polices advertising
Advertisements must be:
- *Honest*
- *Truthful*
- *Decent*
- *Legal*

Q4

(55)

4. (a) Describe **two** different types of families. = 2 x 4 8
- *Nuclear family – parents and their children*
- *Extended family – parents, children, grandparents,*
  uncles, aunts, cousins
- *Blended – combining families, second relationships*

(b) List **three** physical needs and **three** emotional needs
provided by the family. = (3 x 2) x 2 12

Physical needs
- *Food*
- *Clothing*
- *Shelter*
- *Protection*

Emotional needs
- *Love and understanding*
- *Comfort and security*
- *Skills*
- *Personal relationships*

(c) Describe **three** different types of relationships that can exist within a family. $\qquad$ = 3 x 3 $\overline{9}$

- *Father and mother: adult, organiser of family, financial, equal, loving, respectful, trusting*
- *Father and children: discipline, caring, provider, affectionate*
- *Mother and children: discipline, caring, provider, affectionate*
- *Sibling: sharing, playing, co-operating, respectful*

(d) Outline the **rights** and **responsibilities** of children within the family. = (3 x 3) x 2 $\overline{18}$

Rights

- *Love and understanding*
- *To be cared for*
- *Receive an education*
- *Protection from cruelty and neglect*

Responsibilities

- *Respect parents*
- *Take care of personal space*
- *Do chores/homework*
- *Play with siblings*

(e) Explain the term **norms**. = 2 x 4 $\overline{8}$

Expect a definition of norms and an example
Definition: an acceptable way of behaving in society
Example: attending school, good manners, standing for the National Anthem, etc.

Q5

(55)

5. (a) List the safety guidelines which should be followed in order to prevent a fire in the home. = 5 x 3 $\overline{15}$
   - *Use a fire guard around an open fire*
   - *Never put hot ashes into a plastic bin*
   - *Do not air clothes beside an open fire*
   - *Only move portable heaters when switched off*
   - *Switch off and unplug electrical appliances at night*
   - *Never smoke in bed*
   - *Do not leave frying pan unattended*

(b) Name **three** pieces of fire safety equipment suitable
for use in the home.   = 3 x 3   9
  ● *Fire blanket*
  ● *Fire alarm*
  ● *Fire guard*
  ● *Fire extinguisher*

(c) Outline the procedure that should be followed to ensure
the safety of the occupants of the house in the event of
a household fire.   = 4 x 3   12
  ● *Stay calm, alert all occupants in the house*
  ● *Make sure everybody vacates the house*
  ● *Close doors and windows if possible*
  ● *Do not re-enter the house once it has been vacated*
  ● *Call the fire brigade from outside (mobile or neighbour's phone)*

(d) Describe the first aid treatment for a major burn or scald.   = 4 x 3   12
  ● *If clothing is on fire, wrap a blanket around victim*
    to extinguish flame
  ● *Do not remove any items of clothing stuck to the body*
  ● *Cover exposed burn areas with a clean, dry cloth to*
    stop infection
  ● *Treat for shock – raise the legs and loosen tight clothing*
  ● *Cover the victim to prevent heat loss*
  ● *Get medical help*

(e) Explain why water should **not** be used to extinguish
a fire caused by an electrical fault.   7
Water is a conductor of electricity.
The electricity can travel up the water and cause a shock
to the person trying to extinguish the fire.

Q6

55

6. Wool is a popular natural fibre.
  (a) Give **three** other examples of natural fibres.   = 3 x 4   12
    ● *Silk*
    ● *Cotton*
    ● *Linen*

(b) Name **two** types of wool fabric.   = 2 x 3 $\overline{6}$

- *Gaberdine*
- *Jersey*
- *Tweed*
- *Serge*
- *Flannel*
- *Crepe*
- *Velour*

(c) Sketch a care label suitable for a wool jumper.

Expect the label to contain four of the following points.
Each point should have one explanation.   = 4 x 5

1. *Washing –*	*40°C machine wash*
	Hand wash
	Delicate cycle
	Wash dark colours separately
2. *Drying –*	*Do not tumble dry*
	Dry flat
3. *Dry Cleaning –*	Ⓟ
4. *Ironing –*	*Cool iron*
5. *Bleaching –*	*Do not bleach*

Information should be contained in a box   = 1 x 2 $\overline{22}$

(d) Describe a fabric test that could be carried out in order
to identify wool.   = 3 x 5 $\overline{15}$

Apparatus: *Bunsen burner, tongs, metal tray, wool fibres, matches*
                 May include diagram to illustrate above

Method: *Heat the wool fibres and observe.*

- *When approaching the flame, the fibres will stick together and curl away from the flames.*
- *When burning, the fibres burn slowly and then quench.*
- *The burning fibres smell like burning feathers.*
- *The residue is soft dark ash.*

How to create your own study plan

1 Use the headings in this revision guide to create a list of topics which you want to revise. Begin your list with the topics that you like best.

2 Using the grid on the following page, fill in the names of each topic in the order in which you want to revise.

3 Pick a fixed time each day or week to revise Home Economics and fill in the time and date in the grid.

4 For each topic in your list make your own revision notes. Include key headings, explanations and labelled diagrams.

5 As you complete each topic, tick it off in the boxes in the contents list to record what you have achieved.

6 When you have worked through your list, remember to revise each topic again.

7 In the 'Night before' section of the grid, create a list of the topics which you feel you need to revise on the night before the exam.

Date			
Time			
Section to be revised			

Date			
Time			
Section to be revised			

Date			
Time			
Section to be revised			

Date			
Time			
Section to be revised			

Date			
Time			
Section to be revised			

Date			
Time			
Section to be revised			

Night before exam

Sections to be revised

Higher Level, Section A, Q1

List four foods that are a good source of high biological value protein.

(i) _____ (ii) _____

(iii) _____ (iv) _____

Higher Level, Section A, Q2

Name two fat soluble vitamins and two water soluble vitamins.

FAT SOLUBLE VITAMINS WATER SOLUBLE VITAMINS

(i)_____ (i)_____

(ii)_____ (ii)_____

Higher Level, Section A, Q3

Suggest four ways of reducing the intake of sugar in the diet of teenagers.

(i) _____

(ii) _____

(iii) _____

(iv) _____

Higher Level, Section A, Q4

Explain each of the following terms displayed on food packaging:

(i) best before date _____

_____

(ii) use by date _____

_____

Higher Level, Section A, Q5

Give two effects of heat on milk.

(i) _____

(ii) _____

Higher Level, Section A, Q10

List four items of information that should be included in a letter of complaint to a retailer.

(i) _____

(ii) _____

(iii) _____

(iv) _____

Ordinary Level, Section A, Q1

List four sources of fibre in the diet.

(i) _____ (ii) _____

(iii) _____ (iv) _____

Higher Level, Section A, Q1

Suggest four factors that influence a person's food choices.

(i) _____

(ii) _____

(iii) _____

(iv) _____

Higher Level, Section A, Q5

Explain the term cross contamination _____

_____

_____

_____

Higher Level, Section A, Q6

Give two reasons why food is processed.

(i) _____

(ii) _____

Higher Level, Section A, Q8

Name two voluntary deductions that can be taken from an employee's gross income.

(i) _____

(ii) _____

Higher Level, Section A, Q9

Give two functions of the Consumers' Association of Ireland.

(i) _____

_____

(ii) _____

_____

Higher Level, Section A, Q10

List four state services paid for by taxation.

(i) _____ (ii) _____

(iii) _____ (iv) _____

Higher Level, Section A, Q15

Give two different examples of positive peer pressure among teenagers.

(i) _____

_____

(ii) _____

_____